The
Flight
of a
Lifetime!

*A Journey of Discovery for a
Person of Importance . . . YOU!*

Robert C. Perks

SPARROW PUBLISHING

Published by:

Sparrow Publishing
88 North Pioneer Avenue
Shavertown, Pa. 18708-1024

Edited by: Caroline Braun
Cover Design & Illustration: Lightbourne Images, Copyright 1997
Interior Design: Sans Serif, Inc.

Robert C. Perks
The Flight of a Lifetime
ISBN 0-9657935-2-4
Library of Congress Catalog Card Number: 97-067739

Produced, printed and bound in the U.S.A.

*This book is dedicated first to God for the gift of choice,
a life of love and forgiveness.*

*To my wife Marianne, for staying by my side, unwavering love
and constant belief in me. You are my inspiration and
my strength and have my love
"Ever more".*

*To my two sons Keith and Evan, who are my hope for the future.
Two bright and shining stars in the darkest hours of my life.*

*To my "Pop"and brother Tom, who showed me by example,
the results of hard work and commitment.*

*To Bob Butts, a friend who lives life as if his only mission here
is to give without question, serve without glory,
and love without expectations.
He believes in me.*

*Mr. Mike Pesta for seeing in me
what I could not.*

A special tribute to
Og Mandino

I could not have written this book without acknowledging the influence Og Mandino has had on my life. His writing had a certain magic that would take me away from the worries of the day and transport me into the lives of his characters. Every book had a purpose, a message that, if applied to your life, could change you forever. I remember that whenever I finished one of his books I always needed to stop for a few minutes so I could let go. He took me places that I didn't want to leave. His stories seemed so real that I wanted to believe they were true. I know that I can go back any time I need to just by reading his books again. But there were so many more places he could have taken me.

Even though you will be a part of me forever . . .
I will miss you, Og!

Contents

1 ❖

Thanks God,
for Unanswered Prayer

"*D*ead at 46, buried at 80." I read that line somewhere and tucked it away until now. I remember that it referred to a man who had given up long before he died. My only problem is, in my mind, I may be dead and buried at 46. I have lost my will to live. I feel what I believe is right, but life is asking for something more of me. I don't think I want to go that direction. It's just not me.

There's one thing in this world you can count on. Change. The world and everything in it will be different tomorrow. That includes you. The most difficult part you might think would be keeping up with it. I've found liking the changes to be the biggest challenge.

But like it or not, life goes on.

I'd like to blame all of this on a mid-life crisis. But I'm afraid I've been down this road too many times before. "It's not the problem, it's how you react to it." I read that somewhere before, too. I guess I've chosen the wrong reaction because right now I don't care to go on. I've chosen to be a failure. They say, though, that failure is an event not a person. But at this moment I feel like a fail-

1

ure, act like a failure and, after a time, my depressing inactivity probably will help me to smell like a failure.

My name is Christian Tyler. I am a professional speaker by trade. That was the way I thought, felt and acted until one day I understood that I was right where I had chosen to be. What I'm about to share with you is somewhat unbelievable. But as my wife, Michele always says, "You better get your believer fixed."

Six years ago, before becoming a speaker, I had reached a peak on my career path and at that point in my life I was making the most money I had ever made. But I hated the job and it showed. I was working for a religious order as a fundraiser and they fired me. Fired by nuns. How bad can you be to be fired by nuns?

This kind of experience is easier when you are young. I had just turned 40. This was devastating. A few years before I had gone through a divorce. It was my decision and a very unpopular one among all my friends and family. Oh, blame it on approaching 40, the devil made me do it, or just another turn my life needed to take, but in this day and age placing the blame elsewhere in your life is a very popular thing to do. We analyze what's wrong with us and then blame it on everyone else. Your teacher in second grade embarrassed you. Your mother was overbearing. Your father wasn't loved when he was a child so he didn't love you. That's why you do what you do.

But, in reality, who I was at that moment in life was my choice. We are a total summation of all of the choices we've made. Thus, "It's not the problem, it's how we react to it." I was not successful because I chose not to be successful.

The pressures in my life at that particular moment seemed unbearable. Prior to losing my job I had separated from my first wife, then divorced, remarried, bought a new home, hit the big 4-0 and then I lost my job just before the holidays.

I saw a test for this once. I am sure if I took it right

then my score would be far beyond the 300 maximum for being on the verge of a major breakdown. I was.

At first, going on unemployment right around the holidays seemed like a terrible thing. But it soon became very comfortable to think I could enjoy my favorite time of year at home with plenty of free time to soak in the feel and aroma of Christmas.

I selectively sent out resumes to the places I felt would benefit from my many years of experience. They would be thrilled to know I was available. Besides, everyone always makes career changes right around the new year. Jobs would be plentiful. Or so I thought. But this was the year we all added a new word to our vocabulary. Downsizing. The employment lines were filled with mid-management people who were dumped in an effort to cut costs. The corporate world became too big around the middle and desperately needed a diet plan. Trimming mid management became the tool for survival for many businesses. It was like a disease spreading across America. You could ask anyone if they were affected by downsizing, and they could easily name family or friends who had lost a job or taken a lesser position with their company just to survive.

For me, knowing all of that to be true didn't make a difference. You see, I was convinced that it was only me who was dealt this horrible blow. For some reason, life had chosen me to crap on and I deserved it. I spent day after day wallowing in my pity. Most mornings I couldn't care less if I got up. Many nights I couldn't fall asleep. I hated the night time. It always gave me the opportunity to review my life and reinforce my self image as a failure.

I remember praying to God to take my life.

This day began like all of the rest. I slithered out of bed cursing the day; at the same time glad to be out of the darkness of the much-hated night. Unfortunately I always carried that darkness with me throughout the day. It was in my heart and soul. It clouded my thinking, dampened my spirit and darkened every conversation I had with my wife.

As I forced myself to face this day, I felt something different. It was the extra dose of doom and gloom I fed myself the night before. I truly dreaded beginning this day. There was no purpose, no meaning to my life. I was merely existing. I was like a leech sucking every last ounce of beauty out of my world and replacing it with thoughts of death. I dragged myself through the routine of making coffee, turning on "Regis and Kathie Lee" and getting the paper from the front porch. My day began and ended just by looking in the want ads section of the newspaper. If it did not offer any opportunities for employment, my day was basically over. I gave up sending out blind letters of introduction to companies not advertising for help. It was a shot in the dark and produced no results. It wasn't like the old days. You would send a resume and not only get a "thanks for applying" letter but, if you were selected for an interview, they sent regrets if they hired someone else. Now they never acknowledge hearing from you at all.

Well, this day had ended shortly after beginning. I had just finished my coffee. I always drank from the same cup, a hand-painted stoneware of shades of blue and white. It had an ocean scene of sailing ships and rocky coast line. A leftover from my previous marriage. I used it as a motivator to remind me of things I love in life, the hopes of one day living near the ocean where I can turn my back on the world if I so desired. But today those images only reminded me of shipwrecked dreams and sunken treasures far beyond my reach. As I walked back into the living room, newspaper in hand, it all came rushing in on me. Thoughts of failure and defeat. The man who walked out on his kids. The guy with the big plans and hopes for a bright future with a new bride. The man who was weaving the same familiar dreams, talking the big talk to a spouse ten years younger than him. I was a liar, a cheat, and certainly not the man I wanted to be at 40 years old.

I looked toward the ceiling. Tears began to stream down my face. I had been asking God to take me from all of this for weeks now. No, *begging* Him to. There were so many who deserved a second chance at life, but not me. I wanted him to take my life and spare someone with greater potential than me.

But this time my prayer was different. It was simple. I screamed at the top of my lungs, "God help me!" Then, from a standing position, I fell directly to my knees and sobbed like a lost child.

My head touched the floor as I bent over crying. I heaved the cry and moan of a man desperate for life yet longing for death. I slowly rolled to my right side in the curved, comforting fetal position, still pouring my heart out onto the floor.

My dog Daisy, an Old English Sheepdog mix we had adopted from the S.P.C.A., came crawling to my side sensing that something was very wrong. It's an amazing bond that is created between owner and dog. A dog can learn every mood of it's owner, and no matter who you are that day to everyone else, the animal longs for your touch and approval and gives so much more in return.

Daisy's presence was so comforting. For the next few minutes we lay there like a child and favorite stuffed animal. Silent, motionless, deep within the moment, rested to a near point of blissful sleep I heard a voice. *"Ever more"*, it said, whisper-like. *"Ever more."* Again I heard it, softly muffled. It startled me, as if someone had whispered in my ear. I opened my eyes but saw no one. My dog, still curled next to me and unaffected by the sound, woke to my restlessness.

Suddenly I remembered an experience as a young child, about ten years old. My friends and I had been playing near the railroad tracks that ran about a block from my home. This was the border line which my father had designated as off limits. However, being a curious child, I had often crossed the tracks, full of fear, but the lure of the forbidden land filled my soul with excitement every time.

There was an old abandoned building we often broke into. For young adventurous boys it served as a bombed-out retreat for soldiers of war, a prison, spook house ride at Halloween, and a secret club house.

That day, several of my friends and I were playing just outside the building. We were making plans of attack on our enemy when suddenly we heard a moan from inside. At first we dismissed the sound as wind blowing through the building. Then, once again, we heard it. It was an awful sound of desperation. We gathered near the old wooden door and slowly pulled it open.

One by one we entered the dimly lit room. Brave as we seemed at the moment, it wouldn't take much for us all to scatter in panic. Off in the corner, propped against the wall, was a man seated on what appeared to be our treasure chest. It was an old wooden soda crate we creatively adapted to our needs.

We stood silently until once again he moaned a tremendous gasp, this time reaching out his hand.

Instantly my friends scrambled for the door, screaming. I stood frozen in place.

Slowly I approached the man, getting close enough to see he could do me no harm. He wasn't very big. His dirty clothes seemed to hang on his thin shallow frame. His face was creased and dry from overexposure to life and undernourishment. Still not a word having passed between us, he looked up at me and raised his hand to his mouth, trying desperately to moisten his parched lips with his tongue. He was thirsty. I ran out the door and headed toward my home. Mom was working in the kitchen as I opened the refrigerator and grabbed the container of Kool Aid® and sprinted for the door. My mother stopped me just inches from escape with unwanted questioning. She handed me paper cups and a stack of her freshly baked chocolate chip cookies. Then she praised me for sharing with my friends. If she only knew.

I ran as quickly as possible back to the building. I was sure the man thought I had abandoned him. As I placed the feast in front of him he gently raised his head and looked into my eyes. A single tear ran down his face as he reached for a drink. He never said a word. I asked him his name several times, struggling to make conversation. Each time he muttered a word that was almost unintelligible. All I could make out was what sounded like *"Ever more"*, again and again. What kind of name was that? What did he mean, "Ever More?"

The dinner hour was approaching and I needed to return home. I told the man to leave everything and I would be back tomorrow. I knew that this meal wouldn't get him very far, so I reached into my pocket and rummaged through the little change I had: three nickels, two pennies, a half stick of gum, and my lucky half dollar. My grandfather had given this coin to me when I was younger. It was a 1943 Liberty half dollar. He always made a joke out of it. There is a woman pictured on the coin, and in the lower left the sun is beaming its light upward. He would say, "Do you know that this lady is married? There's her little son." On the reverse there is an eagle, and under its left wing is a heart etched by my Gramps. I had promised I would always keep this coin. But at the moment this man needed it more. I set it down on the crate and told him it was lucky, waved good-bye and headed for home. Upon my return the next day I found that the man had moved on. There upon the crate was our container and, wrapped around the handle, a leather strip—somewhat like a suede shoelace. It had been made into a bracelet, with six colorful beads tied together and knots at both ends. At 10 years old this was truly a treasure. I have kept that bracelet until today, and

I have thought about the man often. But I have not heard *"Ever more"* again until now.

I brushed it off as if it were a part of a dream. But this wouldn't be the last I would hear these words.

It took time for me to return to reality. But as I slowly sat up, Daisy still by my side, I realized how relieved I was. I somehow felt cleansed. I had cried like I had never cried before, from deep inside my soul.

I realized afterwards that I had reached a breaking point. Like a pressure cooker ready to explode. The simple act of changing my prayer to God from "take me" to "help me" began a transition in my life that would guide me through even more difficult times ahead.

In the next few weeks there were no burning bushes or other miracles to mark my future path through life, but I had a keen awareness of a change that had taken place. I was totally convinced that God had a plan for me. Somehow it would be revealed.

I wasn't raised to believe that miracles still take place. My religion bored me. It never inspired me or excited me to take on life and its challenges knowing that God was beside me. I had attended church because I was supposed to attend. It wasn't until I was older, when a renewal was sweeping many of the churches, that I learned about the Holy Spirit and realized It was as much alive today as It was in the Bible. There was always excitement during the meetings held in the basement of the church. You never knew what was going to happen when the Holy Spirit took over. God was alive and well and very much a part of each of us.

My church now is anywhere I am at the moment. My God is forever in my heart. I've come to accept the thought that we are not human beings trying to be spiritual, but spiritual beings struggling to be human. It is my humanness that is my downfall. The lessons learned from my born-again days stay with me. Every once in a while, my wife and I will search out a spirit-filled congregation.

We'll participate until they spend more time dancing then praying, and then we return to my home-based church, the "Hour of Power" with Robert H. Schuller. He broadcasts worldwide with a message of hope. Dr. Schuller helps me to apply the Bible to my everyday life. His "possibility thinking" is as much a part of my planning as my faith in God. My experiences in faith have taught me that I'll never hear that deep resounding voice of God speaking from the heavens telling me: "Christian Tyler, go to the north and find your future there! This is God. You better listen!" No, God is that small soft voice deep within me. I always thought it was me talking to myself. But it was God responding to my thoughts.

When I'm not paying attention to that voice, God sends people into my life. I found that out the hard way. Always, after stumbling and falling on my face, I would discover the obvious answer right in front of me. So I've adopted this new attitude. When I'm looking for answers, I first search within myself. Then I search for them in others. God is always sending people to me with messages. No, they don't come knocking at my door like Western Union. In fact they don't even know they have a message for me. I just listen intently to everyone I speak with. Upon their approach I silently ask, "Are you the one?" I know that if I said it out loud they would probably put me away.

The benefits of this are incredible. Because I've become such a good listener, I've gained powerful stories from perfect strangers. Stories that I've shared at just the right moment during a speech.

Many of my best messages have come from people I have met on the plane while traveling from one engagement to another. One of my favorites is a story about a woman I met on a short flight from Pittsburgh to Atlanta. I had the aisle seat just behind first class. I had just settled in when I noticed one of the last passengers to board was a woman who appeared to be in her 60s accompanied by a five year old. Please forgive me, but the last thing I want sitting next to me on an airplane is a rambunctious five year old. I've had this experience before. The parent usually nods off knowing they have a built-in baby sitter strapped in place with nowhere else to go. If I have to have a child next to me I prefer my own. That may sound mean and totally unlike the loving, caring, emotional guy I think I am. But flight time is work time for me. Or, at the very least the only chance I have to catch up on sleep.

Well, this experience turned out to be wonderful. As the woman approached, ticket in hand, I knew as she paused at my row that she had a story to tell. I could see it in her face. Her steel-gray eyes caught my attention. There's a marble-like look in the eyes of youth, that softens as the years pass. The whites of her eyes seemed soft as egg whites. But the steel gray remained sharp. My son, Kile, has the same distinct color, and it's very appealing. Steel gray is an appropriate description as her eyes cut right to my heart. Usually I am lost for conversation when I first look at eyes like these. I stutter and fumble for words.

This time, however, I was comforted.

We started out with basic chit chat. "Where are you going?" "Is it a vacation?"

I found out that this was her grandchild and they had been visiting Pittsburgh. The next few moments were quiet as the crew prepared for take-off. This is the moment when thoughts of a recent plane crash on take-off always stirs the stomach and raises the heart beat.

The young child sat quietly watching out the window as the ground crew loaded the last few bags. As we approached the runway the woman turned to me and asked what I did for a living. "I'm the luckiest man in the world. I get paid to tell people they're important. I'm a motivational speaker," I said proudly. She smiled, nodded, seemingly unimpressed.

We had been flying about 20 minutes when she

turned to me and said suddenly, "My husband died just last year." I offered my sympathy. "Do you know what my biggest regret is?" she asked. "We didn't take time to play. We did all the things we were supposed to do. He worked hard all of his life. We both did. We were so busy becoming, never getting there." She stopped for a moment gathering her thoughts. I said nothing. "We just never took time to be silly," she said matter-of-factly. How sad that was, having regrets. I call them the "shoulda dones". I shoulda done this when I had the chance.

If I had not spoken with her I would never have learned a valuable lesson. In listening to the people around you, you also get direction in life. Prior to the moment when the world came crashing down on me, all I ever did was ask for things from God. He sent messages to me. But I was waiting for the thunder and roaring voice.

Sometimes the most noticeable sound is a whisper. *"Ever more"*

2 ❖

New Beginnings

New days bring new prospects when you are on the path to a better life. It's an incredible feeling. It's like taking a trip to a new place. Your road map and the signs along the way confirm that you have taken the right roads and all the tricky turns. The excitement is as much in the journey as the destination.

Today I started out on a new journey. I had reached a crossroads in my life at mile marker #40 that required certain standards be met before I could continue. By now I should have 2.3 kids, a house on the corner in some fancy development, a retirement plan, and my spouse should be working for the government. I would be closer to my gold watch, and should be hanging around the mall with the other old guys. Traditional standards had long been abandoned by corporate America in lieu of higher profits and low employee morale. But still, certain goals in life were written in stone by generations before us.

Today, in spite of the fact the headlines of every major paper proclaimed this the worst unemployment in decades, I chose to stay focused on what I expected from life, not what life expected from me. I needed to make changes. I needed a miracle.

My prayers were about to be answered in the form of a

250-pound bear of a man who was about to change my life with just four words.

A few weeks had passed since that incredible day that re-awakened my will to live. I had taken the first steps to dust off my dreams and make plans for the future. I simply decided to take one day at a time.

I had been trying to play catch-up with all of my bills. I had come to know most of my bill collectors by their first names. That was my way of handling the embarrassment attached to the seemingly insurmountable debt I had accumulated in recent years. Most of the collectors were just trying to do their job—although I am convinced one woman I dealt with chews on bones in between collection calls.

I didn't like not paying my bills on time. I disliked even more being treated like a criminal just because I fell behind on payments. This conflict needed to be resolved and I was the one who had to do it. I used this problem as the driving force, the motivation to change my life. We all like to avoid conflict. But conflict is a part of life. Our world is filled with natural conflicts such as day into night, summer into fall, and youth into old age. We need to turn these conflicts into positive forces. But many of us fear conflict as much as we fear change. This stems in part from unresolved conflicts in our past. Or the feeling of an inability to deal with conflict because it appears to be bigger than us. "You can't fight city hall!" There comes a time when we must face our fears or be controlled by them. Until now I had given control of my life over to the fear of failure. But no more.

I had been a credit union member for about ten years. There was always one gentleman I dealt with at the UFCW Federal Credit Union. His name was Mike Pesta. Meeting Mike for the first time you would think he was a little too serious about what he does. In fact, he is. He's serious about straightening out your financial life. He takes great pride in attacking other financial institutions, finance companies in particular, that make it too easy to get loans and credit cards. Finance companies then charge interest rates of 20% and up.

Credit Unions are non-profit organizations owned by their membership who have a say in how they operate. Each state in the United States has a league or Credit Union System with local chapters that meet to plan and shape the future of what they call the "movement". Mike is a walking, talking example of the ideals set forth by the original founders of the movement. The image of the "Little Man" (a man carrying an umbrella) symbolizes the protection of his Credit Union. The founders believed that a person's character was as important as his financial ability to repay. That's what Mike still believed.

That almost sounds like pioneer America. Taking a person for his word; trust based on character. Mike lived those ideals every working day. He has a heart bigger than he is, and he's pretty big.

Everything about Mike is round. His arms slope gently from his rounded shoulders. His circle-like face is accented by a healthy-size nose that supports a pair of glasses almost magnifying his eyes. His strong, massive hands disappoint you in a hand shake. He barely squeezes, maybe over-compensating because of his size. It's the first indication of the gentleness inside. Don't get me wrong, he's no wimp. In fact, get a few drinks in him and he'll tell you jokes that will curl your hair.

I hadn't seen Mike in many years. I wasn't sure if he would even remember me. But I made an appointment to meet with him. I needed his help desperately.

During the drive over, I practiced my song and dance. What could I tell him that would make sense? I was way in debt and unemployed. My only income came from a state unemployment check about a fourth of my regular salary. How could I ever pay a new loan?

As I pulled up across the street from his office, still rehearsing my speech, I hesitated for a moment. I thought,

"I will never get a loan." I opened my door and as I took one step out I heard, "Christian! Hello. I'm glad to see you." It was Mike.

I suddenly felt uneasy, off balance as he approached. There we were face to face. "How are you, Christian?" he asked in his deep very recognizable voice. "Not too good,", I confessed.

"Christian, anything you want just ask," he said.

That stopped me cold. I was confused and relieved. It's what I wanted to hear but shocked that he said it.

"Christian, I've watched you through the years. I've seen your picture in the paper and I watched you when you worked for the PBS television station," he said. "I know one day you're going to be a success and I want to be a part of that success." Typically Mike.

Then he said the words that absolutely changed my life. "I want you to know that *I believe in you,* Christian." POW. He stopped me dead in my tracks. I was speechless.

"I believe in you!" Next to the words "I love you," they must be the most important words you can say to someone. We've all seen the look on the face of someone struggling in life. Many times it's for a kind word or gentle touch in mere recognition of their existence.

Mike's words lifted me up. He believed in me. He could see something I couldn't, and I wanted to believe too.

Well, I got that loan. My life was back on track financially. But where was I going?

I was about to finally discover my life's purpose. A man with a mission. It would all come about by giving away the only real thing I had. Me.

3 ❖

Giving Yourself Away

"You'll get what you want out of life if you help
enough people get what they want."

Zig Zigler

*I*t was time for me to stop holding this
pity party. Time had come to take
control of my life. My future began
yesterday and I'm always one step behind. I have a great
deal of catching up to do.

My job for now was finding a job. The market was
bleak and opportunities were few. So I needed to keep
myself busy with a project. Every day I read more stories
of despair. The news reports on television always featured
another company downsizing and more plant closings.
The lines at the unemployment office were growing
longer. I decided that as much as I needed help I also
needed to offer help. When you think you've nothing to
give, you can always give yourself away. What value can
one place on skills, ideas, and experience?

A great example of this is our volunteer system
throughout the world. People giving of themselves in

hospitals, nursing homes, schools, non-profit organizations like the American Red Cross. Many of these organizations could not exist without the time donated by everyday ordinary people from all walks of life. Perhaps it's serving in your church as a greeter or as the clean-up crew for the annual spaghetti dinner. And just as important is the guy who shovels the next door neighbor's walk because he's out of town. Or the pot of soup someone makes when the man across the street passes away and the family needs to prepare for the onslaught of visitors from out of state.

There wasn't a better time or place for someone to help all of the unemployed. But what could I do? What one thing did we all need to get through this? Hope.

If you want to start a business, find a need and fill it. So I decided to sell the unemployed hope. I had spent enough time wandering around our local mall to realize that centralized shopping, everything under one roof, made the mall concept so popular. If you were looking to change your life and you needed many choices, where would you go?

My answer was a one-day conference/seminar on employment opportunities. It wasn't to be a job fair, but an informational resource. I called together all the agencies, colleges and seminar leaders I could find. Before I knew it, I had signed up 25 vendors and scheduled six speakers. The speakers would present topics such as goal setting, interview skills, change, and how to dress for success. The seminar was to be free. The local papers publicized it. Television and radio promoted it, and over 1,000 people attended.

I needed to tell those who attended my story so that they would know we all shared in this experience. My message needed to come from my life experiences, and they needed to feel my compassion. This talk had to come from my heart not from a punched out, prepared speech.

The night before the event I toiled with diagrams and notecards so I would not forget the points I wanted to make. My experience as a PBS membership director on air for fundraising telethons had prepared me to babble on forever, but my time with them at this seminar would be brief. I needed something powerful.

As I looked through my bookcase trying to find a best-seller they might be familiar with, I came across my Bible. The zippered book cover looked old and tattered but I knew the inspiration inside was timeless. As I opened the cover, the old leather bracelet from my childhood fell onto the table. I remembered the man who had given it to me in trade for the kindness I had shown him. What a powerful story this would make. I wanted to remind everyone not only how important it is to help those in need, but how gracious it is to permit someone to help you when you are in need.

I had found just what I had been looking for. I would recreate the bracelet and assign a meaning to each of the colored beads. This would help me to illustrate to those at the seminar how very important they were. It would become my "I believe in you" bracelet.

The words and description came easily to me:

"I Believe in You Bracelet"

What the beads represent:

Clear Bead:
Your future is whatever you want it to be. All of the possibilities are clearly within your reach.
Blue Bead:
Calm, tranquillity, peace of mind are all part of the decisions you make that are right for you.
Red Bead:
The heart. The center of your life is love. You give it, and are surrounded by it. No matter what, you will always have mine.

Yellow Bead:
Sunshine, warmth, a bright future. On days that are
the darkest, your faith is like a beacon in the night. Be
strong when the world expects weakness.
White Bead:
Purity, cleansing. Each day is a clean white canvas.
Each decision, a stroke of the brush. You are the artist.
Your life is your masterpiece.
The Knots:
The two that hold the beads represent your ability to
hold it all securely together with confidence.
The Knots and the Pink Bead at the bottom:
These represent the adjustments you need to make in
order to reach your goals. The pink bead is the beauty
of a sunset at the end of each day.

*Do not count the harvest. Count the seeds that you
planted, one day at a time!*

This event was the effort of many, and a dream come
true for me. But it was much like my childhood Christmas holidays. I was always so eager for that special day to
arrive. If I could, I would have magically traveled through
time and space to get directly to Christmas Day. But oh!
The day after. Now I would have to wait another 365
days!

This program was over. No matter how hard I tried
there wasn't another day on my present calendar that
would come close to the excitement this one provided. So
what next?

The local media soon forgot who I was and what had
been accomplished. Hopefully, the people who had attended made some choices and planned the changes nec-
essary to accomplish their new-found goals. At least some
of them did, I was sure of it. There were so many people
from upper and mid management. One man, whom I had
admired and respected for years, had approached me dur-

ing one of the breaks. I thought for sure he was there representing the bank he worked for as branch manager. In fact, he was looking for work. He was in his mid-fifties, and the prospects for finding work at this point in his life were dim.

I remember him telling me that he was a fighter, a survivor. Nothing would hold him back. In fact he said that when he got to his next management position I was to look him up. He wouldn't hesitate to hire me. But he was sure I would get loads of offers because of my exposure during this project.

But did I? Even with all the attention and the positive feedback I got from friends, there wasn't a single opportunity presented to me. I found myself once again wandering aimlessly around the local mall.

On one such occasion, while seated in the food court, about a month after the seminar, trying desperately not to run into anyone I knew, I heard, "Christian, how are you?" The voice sounded familiar. It was an old friend from the not too distant past. " Stan, how good it is to see you," I replied. Stan was a local police officer, now turned detective. Our friendship went back to my restaurant days when I worked as a manager and Stan would always stop by for coffee. Great guy. He always gave me the sense that I could trust him with anything. The kind of cop who was dedicated and proud to be a cop.

"So Christian, what are you up to?" he asked. " Well nothing much. I'm in between jobs," I said, using that comfortable phrase instead of "unemployed." "Oh, I heard you were unemployed." So much for comfort. "But I saw you on television when you did that seminar. I told my wife about it and we agreed that was the perfect job for you. You've always been great with people," he said.

I paused for a moment and thought about what he had just said. "Look Christian, if there's anything I can do, just ask. These times are tough for everyone." "You're right, Stan. They are," I said. As we said our good-byes with promises of getting together just like the old days, I couldn't stop thinking about what he had said. The seminar business. God, I love being in front of an audience. But what would I have to offer? How could I get started? The thought of starting a business of my own overwhelmed me. I had no money to invest. Then I could hear Robert Schuller say: "You have no money problems. Only an idea problem." Right. Me in business for myself. Now that's a joke.

"Ever more!"

There it was again. So softly, almost unintelligible. Where is this coming from? Has all of this caught up with me? This must be the break down. I'm over the edge. *"Ever more."* "Stop it!" I shouted. A family passing by looked at me as if I were a lost homeless person whose only friend in life was in a conversation with himself.

I rushed out of the mall and headed for my car. I must have looked like I had stolen something. I could see people turning to look at me. My heart raced as I sat there. I didn't want to drive until I had calmed down. What was going on? I had always believed in the inner voice that often took over when I was trying to make an important decision. God talks to me that way. But this was different. I hadn't shared this with my wife Michele, but perhaps it was time. How would I explain? And what about this new idea of starting a business? This was going to be quite an evening. I could hear it now . . . "So Christian. What's new? How was your day?" she would ask. "Well, I met an old friend today I hadn't seen in a long time. I'm going into business and I'm hearing voices. Would you like more meatloaf?"

I thought this wasn't going to be easy. But I was in for quite a surprise. My life was about to take an incredible turn.

I started preparing dinner as soon as I got home. I selected two nicely marbled delmonico steaks , her favorite. Of course if I really wanted to please her before I told her my story I also had to make homemade mashed potatoes and fresh corn on the cob.

The mashed potatoes have to be just right. After cooking and draining the potatoes, I add some fresh milk and butter, salt and pepper lightly, and add a few slices of Cooper Sharp cheese and a touch of fresh grated Romano. The potatoes should be mashed by hand. It's a personal thing for me. It brings back memories of Sunday dinners as a child. My father would always mash the potatoes with a kitchen tool designed just for that. It had a well worn red handle. I can still hear the muffled clanking sound as he beat the potatoes to a creamy texture, always leaving just a few small lumps as a reminder that this was no instant side dish. It was a measure of my manhood to be able to mash them as quickly as Dad. I can remember struggling with it as a boy after I had insisted I could do it alone. My father's impatience meant he would soon take over the task.

The table set, a bottle of white wine breathing nearby, and a candle lit in the center of the table created the perfect mood. She would enter the kitchen from the back door, carrying her briefcase, empty lunch bag and whatever treasure she purchased along the way that day. There would be a moment of confusion and brief eye contact followed by a smile, a cautious "hello" and then a quick hug when appropriate. Some days it's better to eliminate some of those steps if either of us seems to have had a bad day. We need space; no, breathing room sometimes. We've never really discussed this ritual. It just seems to have fallen into place. Marriage sometimes is like a pair of jeans. You never really are comfortable until the waist expands slightly, the pockets soften so your hand can slip in for change, and your wallet now fits into the worn spot leaving a faded outline on your butt.

Romantic isn't it?

We said our hellos and small talk. She had had a rough day. Michele works for a grass-roots organization as a community representative. Much of her time is spent organizing volunteers on various committees. Their purpose is to provide programs and resources in regards to health and education. It's a difficult job and she would like to move on, but we both know that's not possible now.

"So Hon, how was your day?" I asked. That question always serves as a release valve . It's just like letting a balloon go that has been inflated to the maximum.

"Not bad at all," she said. Great. That's what I was hoping for.

We both sat quietly for a few minutes, enjoying the meal. I could see the candlelight reflecting off her face, gently washing over her golden brown hair. It was such a perfect moment. I really hated to stir things up. She had really been through enough this past year. Now I was about to tell her something that might set her life in a spin. Then just as I was about to speak she said: "Oh, I came across this most incredible thing today. During my afternoon break I was paging through a business magazine and I came across an advertisement in the back." She got up and turned the kitchen light on to find her briefcase. I panicked, thinking she had destroyed the mood. Now I'd have to start all over again. "Here," she said. "Read this ad. You can start your own business as a trainer with this seminar company. The investment is under $500."

"Ever more." There it was again.

I never even looked at the ad. I sat staring at her in amazement. "Christian, what's wrong? Don't you like the idea? I think you'd do great. The ad says that they provide all the training over a two-day period. Of course, the rest is up to you."

I looked down at the magazine. As if in disbelief I grabbed it from her hand. There it was, just as she said. "Which magazine is this?" I flipped to the cover. "Successful Entrepreneur" it said in big gold print.

"Well, what do you think? You give it a try and when you become successful I can leave my job and travel with you," she said.

"OK. OK. I'll call first thing tomorrow," I told her. "But there's something else I need to talk to you about."

"What is it? You look so serious," she said.

"Well, for the last few months I've . . . " The phone rang. I couldn't believe the way things were going.

"Just let it ring," she said. "The answering machine will get it."

Just as I started over again I could hear my son Kevin on the machine. "Hel l l lo. Dad this is me. I just finished my homework and mom is taking me to the mall. So I wanted to call now to tell you *dream about me.*"

"I have to get this," I said rushing to the phone. Ever since my first wife and I divorced, my two sons, eleven-year-old Kevin, and Kile, 19, have always phoned me every day possible to say good night. They live just 15 minutes away, but my day isn't complete until I've spoken to them, even if it's for a few minutes.

"Hi buddy! I'm glad I caught you before you hung up. We were just having dinner. That's why I let the machine get it."

"Sorry, Dad." he said.

"No, you know I wouldn't sleep well tonight if we didn't talk. Is Kile there?" I asked.

"What do you think?" he said with a tone of sarcasm. "He's probably with his girlfriend, as always."

Kevin and I talked until his mom yelled for him. "Dad. I've got to go. I love you. Dream about me."

"I will. I even day dream. Goodnight."

Michele had begun clearing dishes. "What's for dessert?" she asked. Oh no, I forgot dessert. I wanted this meal to be perfect.

"I'm sorry. I didn't have time," I told her. "Wasn't the meal good enough?"

"Yes. It was incredible! What's the occasion?" she asked as she hugged me.

It just seemed all too late to try and explain everything. "I just thought you deserved it," I said.

"Thanks. I needed that."

Later in the evening as Michele went up to bed, I sat in the living room thinking about all that happened that day. I often spent a few minutes by myself just thinking, wondering what was going to happen next. What would tomorrow bring? Or better yet, what will I bring into tomorrow. I had read somewhere that each day is a new chance to start over. My problem was I was spending so much time on what I did wrong the day before, that before I knew it, most of today had past. I have found myself many times apologizing to God for wasting the time He has given me.

Tomorrow, for the first time in months, offered hope. Maybe this would change my life so that happiness would be ours forever more. "Ever more? How ironic!" I said out loud. Michele heard me and shouted down the steps "Who are you talking to, Christian?"

"I have no idea." I replied.

4 ❖

Life is What Happens

*I*t takes commitment and a little insanity to start a business. Commitment might be new to me but I've had plenty of experience with insanity in my life. One crisis after another in recent months has driven me to the edge involuntarily. Not over the edge, mind you, but close enough to realize how fortunate I am. It must be the breath-taking view. For as long as I can remember, my life has been far from perfect. In a sense, maybe I like it that way.

It's been a few years since I attended the special classes to become a trainer. I'm now a behavioral specialist. But to tell you the truth I don't think I really needed a class to learn why people do the things they do. But it has confirmed what I've known all along. Now I can even put labels on them like Analyst, Good Buddy, Artist, and Task Master.

But that's the problem. We label too much. We are all so very quick to pre-judge someone by the color of their skin, the town they live in, the way they dress, or the car they drive. But life has given me a second chance. Or is it my third or fourth? All I know is that all of my life I could see past labels. I was always the kid who made friends with those no one else wanted. I was their protector. I walked to school with the girl everyone made fun of, and along the way I found out she was quite an incredible person. Her family was poor but her spirit was rich with dreams. I watched from afar as my athletic friends got all the girls and I became the class clown. I was slightly overweight because my Mom couldn't control the sugar bowl when she baked her famous chocolate cupcakes with icing a half inch thick. I then grew up always needing the husky size in young boy's clothing. I was always quick with the self-destructive joke for the sake of a laugh. Never completely happy with who I saw in the mirror, even to this day.

But here I am standing in front of complete strangers, sharing my knowledge, using my talents and making a difference. Where did this confidence come from? How can I do a great job when all of my life I acted the clown?

"I believe in you!" I can still hear Mike saying it just like it was the first time. Someone had confidence in me. He could see what I could not. All of the elements of success that lie dormant in each of us suddenly came rushing to the surface. I have a purpose. I became a man with a mission sent by God to remind everyone just how important they really are in life.

Sounds incredible doesn't it? Well it's not. There is a small voice I hear that keeps telling me not to give up. Everyday circumstances place me in the path of someone new who either has a message or needs one. Oh, there are those days when nothing happens. I stay home and self-destruct. It's my choice to do so. As always at the end of that day I find myself, head hung low, telling God how very sorry I am to have wasted this time.

How do I know that voice is God's? My inner voice, all of my life, has been one of a negative tone. The thought that tells me "You can't do that," or "Who do you think you are?"

Even to this day I have quick flashbacks of negative moments in my life where I have said or had done something wrong to someone else. Those are not of God. But His are the gentle nudges that push me toward doing what's right. He speaks to all of us in ways that only we can understand. We were created and the blueprint destroyed, so no one can reach into our deepest soul like God.

Each of us has been uniquely created and designed to fulfill a need. Our timing on earth coincides with so many other events. Each are linked by a series of acts and decisions we all make each day. The whole of humanity rises and falls like the ebb of the tide according to the extent of suffering and joy. When a young teen commits suicide we are all responsible. When an adult kills for the sake of killing we are all lowered to his level when we accept it as the norm. When thousands of people die of starvation just the other side of the world, we are all losers because of their death.

Then on the other hand, when a family is raised from the depth of poverty by a volunteer organization that provides clothing, shelter and food, the level of humanity is raised. When a community unites against racial bigotry and takes a stand for what is right, God Himself lifts us all to a higher standard. We rise together with the loving touch of a stranger reaching down to a fallen soul, and slide backward with each cry of desperation from a broken marriage.

I believe, though, that there is more than a balance of good and evil. The tilt of the measure leans far toward the good. For our true failing lies more in not recognizing our importance. We, for the most part, do not realize how our individual lives contribute to this ebb and flow. We are not all doers fulfilling our mission by organizing, planning and acting upon those goals. For the most part we contribute to life by being the best we can be within the framework that we call our personal life. Doing the best job at work by exceeding expectations of our employer; raising our children to respect life; participating in the democracy we believe in by voting; and finally by humbly lowering our heads in prayer to a Higher Power in grateful recognition of this gift of living another day.

It is that pattern, the everyday stuff of living that makes us a success. We are being watched as a whole by those lost along the way. Together we contribute to the overall success of humanity and share in its benefits. Your uniqueness is like a single stroke of the brush on a fine painting. The true value does not lie in the finished artwork but in the precise placement of each of the strokes.

I have traveled across this country to places I have never been before. Before doing my presentation I am often warned of particular attitudes of the audience. "Be aware of their negativity," I am told. "They are a tough audience stuck in a rut, " they say. Then I walk out and say, "My name is Christian Tyler, and I believe in you! That's how I start all of my speeches, no matter where I go. You'll understand why in just a few minutes. But first I want to tell you I could care less what you do for a living. I'm here to talk to you about you. Because you are the most important person in the world. Your world." I then spend whatever time I have allotted to me convincing them of this through stories of my life and those whom I have met along the way.

There were times during these past few years where I thought all of this had to be a dream. I felt that at any moment I would wake up on the floor next to my dog, wallowing in my tears. This couldn't be real. It all felt too good.

Thus far, among the wonders I have seen are the incredible Rocky Mountains, the plains of Oklahoma, The Ozarks of Arkansas, the beautiful ocean shores of Maryland, and the Badlands of North Dakota. It is in the people that my treasures are found, more valuable than gold. Like the woman from Arkansas who said, "There are no strangers here. Just friends we haven't met." After giving a speech in Texas, a young woman, moved by what I had to say, handed me a note and walked away. It said, "Yesterday is history. Tomorrow's a mystery. Today is a gift. That's why we call it the present."

Have I reached those lofty goals I set for myself when I fought for my life after losing my job? Am I finally coming to my peak in my career? Not even close. The goals have been adjusted along the way. I had from the beginning written them in pencil so that as I came to a significant point I could adjust them to fit the next goal.

It's like setting out on a hike. Your plans initially take you to that peak easily viewed from the bottom of the hill. Then once you get there the view is so exciting you can't help but to go on. Of course, by nightfall you need to return to home or camp securely for the darkened hours. But then, starting over or moving on sets new challenges for the day ahead.

I have so much more to do, and with God as my partner I can't go wrong. My life is smooth and the road direct. All was running exactly as planned until the phone call from my son Kile.

I had seen very little of him in recent months. He had just turned 18, graduated from high school and now was entering college.

As close as we once were, we seemed to have drifted apart. He was a young man now, with dreams and plans of his own. He had set his course and was two months into his art major when I received this call.

"Dad, I had to go to the Doctor yesterday," he said.

"Is this your 18,000 mile check up?" I joked.

"No, I've been having problems with my left leg," he said nervously.

"What's wrong with it, growing pains?"

Then my world stopped dead in its tracks as I heard, "There's a lump and he took X-rays." Then from somewhere beyond me I heard what sounded like *"Ever more"*

5 ❖

Not My Child

No one ever knows what the next 24 hours might bring. The worse thing we can do is to become complacent. There are certain things we take for granted. Waking up is one of them. We just simply expect that when we go to sleep we always wake up. Life owes it to us. We paid our dues yesterday, and the pay off is today. That is until you face life and death head on.

I've never been there. I've been around enough other people who have. Some fought for their lives and won, and others never had a chance. Most of them were either old or at least lived a good portion of their lives. My son was 18.

I can remember calling our doctor. I was at home alone. The receptionist was pleasant and could easily understand my impatience in trying to reach him. She deals every day with calls of an emergency nature. She could sense it in my voice. I was scared and struggling desperately for answers. The doctor was unavailable and would have to return my call.

My mind raced. I tried to convince myself that this was just the result of a bump or bruise. The x-rays would reveal an infection and simple antibiotics would be the answer.

I tried to listen to music in an effort to relax. The song

was Pachelbel Canon. I had played it for Kile years ago and he had learned to love its haunting melody as much as I.

The phone rang and startled me.

"Hello, Christian? This is Doctor Boyer. I wanted to get back to you right away."

"Yes Doctor. Thank you. I just needed to talk to you about Kile's leg," I said.

"I know this is probably just routine work. But you know in this day and age . . . "

"Christian," he interrupted. " I am sending Kile to a specialist who can do a bone scan of his left leg."

"Is this some kind of infection?" I asked.

"This is more than an infection. I need to have someone with more experience take a look," he replied.

" A specialist?"

"Yes," he paused. I could hear him take a deep breath. "Look Christian." His voice got quieter as if he didn't want to be overheard. "Once this is scanned, I strongly suggest that you get him out of here to bigger facilities that deal with tumors like this." Tumors. My God, he said tumors. What was he saying to me? Perhaps I misunderstood.

"A tumor? Are you saying that this is a tumor? Could he have cancer?"

"I can't tell you that until we get further testing," he said with a slight hesitation. There was a long drawn out silence. He was so understanding. He could have brushed me off so he could get to his next patient. But he waited. "Christian there's a great deal we can do to help."

"Yes, Doctor thanks."

My heart was pounding so hard that I could feel every beat. I was dazed and confused. I didn't know where to turn. *My God, don't you dare!* I shouted. *Not my son!* I immediately called Michele at work. I could barely get the words out. She said she would be right home. I must have circled that kitchen a dozen times, pacing back and forth like a caged animal. It seemed like an hour had passed since I spoke on the phone to my wife. At last she got home. I looked at her and wept. The tears poured from our eyes as we held each other closely. We stayed in that embrace long enough to get our thoughts straight. As we walked toward the door I could feel the brisk October wind blowing across my tear-dampened face. It sent a chill through my body. It reminded me of the bleak winter days ahead. It seemed appropriate. It matched the mood of what was to come.

A few restless days went by as we tried desperately to go about our lives. My speaking engagements were at a seasonal peak. Many organizations hold their conferences and training sessions in the Fall. It was probably a blessing. It kept my mind occupied as we awaited the results of several tests on Kile. I called my brother-in-law, Dr. Michael Sheraton, asking for his help. He is a renowned vascular surgeon in the Philadelphia area. He asked his colleagues who they thought would be the best orthopedic surgeon, and they all agreed it was Dr. Charles Werner. My brother-in-law called his office and arranged for us to meet with him.

We live about two hours north of Philadelphia. But on this particular drive it seemed like four. It had been requested that Kile use crutches and stay off of the leg as much as possible. The tumor had weakened the bone to a point that the slightest manipulation could cause it to break. We arrived at Dr. Werner's office and were asked to wait in one of the small conference rooms.

As I sat there waiting for Doctor Werner, Kile stood by the window overlooking downtown Philadelphia. The bright sunlight shone on his face while his body was silhouetted against the window curtains. He seemed so big. A song came to mind that my father had sung to me, "Daddy's Little Boy." But he wasn't little anymore. I saw the figure of a young man standing there. Kile has incredibly thick dark brown hair, and slightly rounded shoulders. He has always been a quiet kid who seemed to internalize everything. He could sit for hours drawing pictures of heroes and monsters. We knew early on that he would be an artist.

Hundreds of images flashed through my mind of Kile's childhood. Then suddenly the door opened.

"Good morning, Mr. Tyler," the doctor said. "And you must be Kile.""

"I have only had a moment to look at the x-rays and test results. This type of cancer, although rare, appears primarily in kids Kile's age."

"Cancer?" I said. "This is cancer?"

"You didn't know it was cancer?" asked the doctor.

"No. This is the first we're hearing this."

"I'm sorry. I thought all of this was discussed earlier. Kile has what appears to be Ewings Sarcoma. It's a cancer which starts primarily in the bone. You can see on this x-ray that the tumor in question seems to be protruding out and into the fleshy part of the leg."

"Are you sure it's cancer, doctor? Is there a chance that it's not?" I asked.

"Of course at this point it's all guessing. But I've seen enough of these to know that this type of tumor is normally cancerous." he said. "I'd like to recommend that you take Kile to Hershey Medical Center. There's an excellent staff there who can handle this. Let me place a call to see if they can meet with you today."

As long as I live I will never forget the moment the doctor left the room. Kile and I were silent. I now stood looking out the window as I watched a city full of people rushing about their day. I couldn't understand how this could be. I didn't know what to say to my son. I was his father and I was supposed to have the answers or at least a bit of wisdom passed down from generation to generation.

I turned to face him and prayed for strength. "We'll beat this Kile. Whatever it is, we'll beat it."

"I know Dad," he said.

Dr. Werner returned with all the tests in hand, a paper with directions to Hershey and a referral letter. "Here Kile, this is a passport to recovery." he said. "There's a great deal of territory to be covered and many decisions to be made. Don't waste any time. It seems early enough to head this off."

We thanked him and headed back on the road to Hershey.

As we drove the two hours to the hospital I couldn't help remembering how many times I had faced cancer before. My mother, former mother and father-in-law, and too many others had fought and lost their battles. But I didn't know one young person until now. My son.

We talked of hope and options right up until we walked into Hershey Medical Center. There was something special about this place that both Kile and I could feel. Everyone we met was so pleasant and positive. They made you feel right at home. I knew that no matter what we heard in the next few weeks Kile would come out a winner and this was the place that could make it happen.

Upon initial examination the doctor there had confirmed what Dr. Werner had told us earlier. He told us that depending on where this tumor was there was a chance that Kile might lose his leg.

I couldn't believe what was happening. I had crossed over somewhere. This wasn't the life I knew before. My career was just taking off and suddenly it all didn't make a difference. Within a two week period my life took a turn and I had no idea where I was going next. It had been only a few years since I lost my job. I finally could look back and see how that tragedy was really one of the best things that happened to me, as I had grown so much from that experience.

But this? This was a real crisis. My son's life was at stake and there would be nothing more important to deal with in my life. My career suddenly meant nothing to me. There were no goals, no mission greater than this.

Kile had just started college and the doctors were now telling him to withdraw and dedicate the next year of his life to fighting this disease. A year didn't seem like much of a sacrifice knowing that it meant getting a lifetime in return.

I didn't realize that, in fact, we had crossed over. We now were a part of a world that we all know exists but know nothing about. The world of sickness and disease and of hope and healing. It's a separate dimension, like a Twilight Zone where its inhabitants all have one thing in common. Survival.

I have seen the telethons so many times and been motivated to send a pledge. I watched images of children and babies waiting for a cure, and seen the faces of families whose commitment was undaunting. I have heard stories of beating the odds and winning the battles. I've read of yard sales, auctions, bake sales and walkathons, all produced and directed like Broadway musicals by volunteers and the patients themselves. I have seen canisters at the checkout of my local grocery store with a photo attached of a neighbor I knew or a face I didn't. But I never dreamed of being a participant.

The hospitals are like fortresses built to protect. From them pour prayers to Gods from people of all faiths and a few who become believers. Once you cross over you can see it like steam pouring out of a nuclear reactor tower. Cries and moans, mixed with joy and happiness, rising into the skies above.

I am here now with stories from the inside. Hoping you never need to cross. But confident that if you do, no matter what the outcome, you'll know that you are not alone.

6 ❖

What are the Odds?

Sixty-five percent chance of survival. Better than fifty-fifty. But not ninety-five to one-hundred percent. That's what the doctor said about Kile. But it's more than a numbers game. It's my son and sixty-five percent doesn't sit well with me.

Kile's doctor had stepped into the waiting room to share the results of the biopsy he had just performed. We had spent days and long nights prior to this, guessing what the outcome might be. There would be no cancer. This is just an infection. The obvious tumor is never a reality when you are dealing with your child's life. Deep in our hearts though, we knew. We always knew. So his words really came as no surprise to any of us. But the sixty-five percent chance of survival hit me hard. I had to ask. He had to be honest.

The waiting room for families of patients in surgery is a large comfortable room with couches and big soft chairs. To one side is a small desk where a volunteer is stationed. He or she takes the patient's name and keeps you informed throughout the procedure. In one corner a television is on with no one apparently watching. But it is a comforting distraction every once in a while. There are several people nervously waiting for results. Every few minutes the phone rings and all heads turn in anticipation. The view from the fifth floor overlooking the town of Hershey is marvelous. One by one various family members stroll to the huge window and stare out at the cars and people below. Off in the distance you can see the "Kissing Tower" located in the heart of the famous amusement park. The enclosed ride takes you to the very top of the tower as it slowly turns, giving you a view of the town through "Hershey Kiss®-shaped" windows. They say there have been a few marriages and proposals performed right there. As I looked at this tower all I could remember was how many times in recent years my wife and two sons had enjoyed a day at that park. Our eyes surely must have seen this hospital from that vantage point.

Now here I stood with my heart breaking, having just heard a surgeon tell me my son has a sixty-five percent chance of survival.

I have reviewed every step along the way to where we are now. Memories have come pouring into my soul, mixing and blending under the pressure until days and events become foggy. There are two doors leading to the surgical area just outside this room. Phone calls and swinging doors keep everyone on edge. As the morning progresses and the coffee becomes stale I have watched families come and go. Doctors have entered the room and sat next to loved ones in semi-private conversation. I've seen smiles and heard laughter from those finally relieved by the reports. Then there are the tears and cries from others with not-so-happy news. Kile's doctor was visibly uneasy and started the conversation with idle chat as I, Michele, Kile's mom and step dad, as well as Kile's girlfriend, gathered around for the news. His mom cried out in a moan felt only by a mother. We have both lost parents and family members to cancer. We have not until this point had any survivors. This hit hard.

After the doctor left we all sat speechless. I motioned for Michele to follow me as I walked slowly down the hall. At the time I couldn't begin to imagine where this was coming from, but I had a complete sense of calmness. It was as if I had heard the report and knew the long-term outcome all in the same moment. Kile would survive.

Every family or patient that we spoke to always told us that the two most important things in fighting cancer are a positive mental attitude, and good nutrition. From the onset Kile took charge of his cancer. He was totally in control of his thoughts. From the moment the doctor told him the news, Kile spoke only of positive results. But it was on one particular day that I believe my son was completely healed of his cancer. The treatments for the next year would only be procedure.

During one of the early hospital stays, prior to beginning treatment, Kile was told of all the side effects this particular protocol had. He was very concerned. Everyone left the room for a few minutes and alone in his thoughts Kile had a talk with God.

When I walked back in the room he was crying. I rushed over to hold him. I will never forget the look on his face. There is a picture of Jesus Christ that I have seen many times before. His eyes grab you. His hair is soft and uncombed. Blood drips down His forehead from the piercing points of the crown of thorns. His eyes are dark and in the corners are tears gently flowing down the sides of his face. But there is a look of joy and peace contrasting the obvious pain He is experiencing. It was that same look that I saw on Kile.

"Kile, what's wrong?" I asked.

"Dad, I just had a conversation with God," he said with the pumping breath of a child crying. "He told me that everything was going to be all right. Every once in a while I could hear a faint voice saying what sounded like

"*Ever more*" It's the oddest thing. I can vaguely remember hearing those same words as I was coming out of anesthesia . It was a man's voice. What does that mean, Dad?"

"It means you have nothing to worry about Kile," I said.

So it wasn't just me. Now, whatever that message is, others are hearing it too. What does it mean?

I knew he had experienced God first hand when he finally said . . . "Dad, just as I heard that, I felt this warm rush all over my body. All the way down into my legs. It was like a burning sensation."

"That, Kile, is the healing power of God," I answered.

I held his hand for a few minutes as I sat on the edge of his bed. I broke the silence by asking,

"He didn't happen to mention my name, did He?" We both laughed as the rest of the family returned. I shared that moment later with them in private.

Sixty-five percent. I couldn't get that figure out of my thoughts. I believed that what Kile had just experienced changed that number to one-hundred percent. That was my faith in God. But my humanness still permitted that figure to haunt me.

We all do this. We give a problem over to God and ask Him to take care of it. We believe He will. But then a hundred times more we take it back through worry and confusion. "Leave it with Me," I could hear Him say. "Yes, God I will. But what if? . . . and why not? . . . and how long?"

If I were a gambler I would first put everything I had on the surest bet I knew. I'd bet anything that Kile was in fact healed that day. But in everyday terms the percentages scared me. But why should they? Even based on the doctor's statistics Kile's chances were better than most risks we take daily.

I hear so many people make excuses for why they haven't reached their goals. *What chance do I have of getting that job? I'm a woman. I don't stand a chance of making it in business.* Statistically speaking your odds of getting struck by lightning twice are better than winning a Powerball jackpot. Yet millions play each week. The average person has a 1 in 250,000 chance of dying in a plane crash and a 1 in 12 chance of being in an auto accident. Which do we fear the most? More Americans are injured on metal cans yearly than by combined effects of mopeds, ATVs, chain saws and minibikes. And you have a 1 in 40,000 chance of being hit by a car while walking. Do we stop walking, driving or flying? No, we're too busy living.

The saddest statistics that confirm our struggle state that more than 300,000 people attempt suicide each year, and over 5,500,000 prescriptions for valium are filled every month.

You are destined to win, designed to succeed, but dead in the water the minute you say "I can't."

Those words never crossed Kile's lips, although this next year would be the toughest test in his life.

7 ❖

I Only Hear Their Laughter

*E*very three weeks, for more than a year, Kile spent several days in the hospital undergoing chemo therapy treatment.

My thoughts always return to the day I asked one mother the dumbest question. "How do you get through this?" You just do.

I have sat in this chair at the end of the hallway so many times. I'm watching them coming and going. Moms and Dads up in the middle of the night taking a break while their child sleeps, if only for a few hours or, worse, a few minutes.

There are new faces, new families I haven't met. There goes one now. A young woman in her sleepwear. Not pajamas. Just comfortable clothes she can rest in and yet be ready at a moment's notice to run down the hall for whatever her child desires. They have a special room just off the center lobby on the 7th floor. It's stocked with soda, chips, pretzels, juice, and ice cream for the kids. When you are on chemo your tastes change. One moment you may be sick and the next ice cream sounds great. As a parent you live for the moment.

Mom's restless. Her days have become routine. Dad is home with the rest of the family miles away, which permits him to see his child infrequently. Mom and Dad don't see each other much any more. The relationship suffers from the same disease that is threatening their child's life. When was the last time they held each other closely? When did they share an embrace that really meant something?

Let me guess. The day the doctor came out of the operating room after performing the biopsy. He slowly approaches the couple. He tells them their child has cancer. She cries quietly at first. Husband and wife embrace as she slumps into his arms. He collapses into her weakened shoulders as the doctor sits patiently. His years of experience tell him they must go through this. They let go of each other for a moment as the doctor reassures them that they will do everything they can.

They hold each other intensely, not realizing that this may be the last moment like this for some time. Their focus will change. They will literally pass each other in the hall as they change shifts or give each other breaks. In between the treatments, when their child is at home, they'll have little time or desire to be the couple they once were. Exhausted, they will lie next to each other in bed, gently nudging each other as they quickly fall asleep in each other's arms. No passion or hot steamy thoughts. Just comfort and peace in knowing they're together for now.

Just down the hall from where I'm sitting a young baby sits in a swing. He's so beautiful and bright eyed even at this hour. His life is off schedule too. He's been here many times before. The first time I saw him I noticed how jaundiced he looked. I have since found out that he's waiting for a organ donor. It's been months now and he still waits, as do so many children and adults. They often die waiting.

In the middle of the night, when I can't sleep, I walk

the halls. I find myself near the playroom just down the hall from the Child Life office. The staff from the office are incredible. They are there to provide programs for the children and the parents. They also serve as a link to all of the services available. They can be your best friend when you just need to talk. Walking outside the playroom, facing a collection of kid-size cars and wagons I stop to look closer at the pictures I've glanced at so many times before.

There's a large photo of a young girl with marker in hand, facing a canvas on which is a masterpiece she has just created. Her head is bandaged much like a turban. Her wrist has the familiar patient ID bracelet, and her hand has a small bandage covering what must have been where the intravenous needle was.

On the wall opposite from where I'm standing are four more very large photos featuring beautiful children at play. One stands out more than the rest because I am most familiar with that look. The child is smiling a great smile while holding a painted pumpkin created by her during some past Halloween season.

She's bald, not like a newborn, but like a cancer patient. So is my son. You get used to it. I'm not sure if they do. But you begin to realize how truly beautiful a person is when their personality out-shines their pain.

I have seen this area crowded and busy with children laughing, playing, and forgetting their circumstances. Mixed in the crowd are moms and dads who forget for a while, too. I sit here at this hour, looking at the toys all neatly lined up in a row waiting for their return. I wonder how many children rode in the wagon? Are they well? Do they remember this spot, this magic room?

I know they remember. I can feel their presence. I swear I can hear them giggle just around the corner near the door.

I've put on some weight since this all started. Some people stop eating when they are stressed. I eat. My other favorite spot at the hospital was the cafeteria. They were open almost 24 hrs.

Sometimes I would go there and sit with a drink in hand and watch and listen to other people.

Doctors, hospital staff and patients' families all blended together during meal time. But during the late night most of the people there were family members. You could see the anguish and pain on the faces of many who took breaks during long recovery periods for their loved ones. They were burned out, scared and lonely.

One evening around ten o'clock I heard the most incredible story. The woman who was stationed at the exit for the parking lot came walking in with a small bouquet of flowers. Her face was beaming with joy. One of the workers made a fuss about a secret admirer.

"You're not going to believe this," she said. "I have all kinds of people who pass through that gate. Many in such a hurry that they don't even acknowledge that I exist. I smile, say hello, and wish them a nice day. You know we have had trouble with the ticket machine at the entrance. Some days it just wouldn't give one. We then go on the honor system. I simply ask everyone how long they were parked there. Most people are gracious and answer as honestly as they can. But one man blew up at me and was outraged. I've heard it all before but this guy was really upset," she laughed as she continued the story. "This went on for several days afterwards. Every time he came up to the gate he would hold his ticket out, look the other way and speed off when the gate opened. Then today, right around dinner time when the traffic is the heaviest, he comes walking toward my booth. He stops the next car in line and says to me, "I have been very rude to you this week." I said, "Yes you have." He then told me that his child was very ill and his life was totally upside down.

"I want to apologize for my rudeness. These flowers are for you!" The woman pauses for a moment and with a quiet whisper and eyes filled with tears she said, "I've never had anyone do that for me before. I have worked in that small booth for ten years, eight-hour shifts, and never had anyone acknowledge me that way."

"What did you do?" asked her friend.

"As he turned and walked away I yelled out to him, 'Can I give you a hug?' He said 'Sure!' And there we stood in the drive, cars backed up down the aisle, hugging each other. I will never forget that moment. He made me feel special."

I know I was supposed to hear that story. You see that man's gesture of love and compassion not only touched her life, but will have far-reaching affects on everyone who hears it. One act of kindness is multiplied a thousand times.

In just a few months I will be gone from here. No longer will I need to be here, wondering, worrying. But there will be others after me. This is a special place, the 7th floor. A child arrives hurt, broken or dying. But this miracle machine called Hershey Medical Center, mixes its magic with a little hope, a great deal of love, and just the right amount of knowledge.

They, with God's guidance and gifts, gave me my son back when cancer crept into our lives. Thanks to all of them for creating a secure, healing, loving atmosphere. You fight hard for life. Most times you win.

But isn't that the way we all should fight? Fight to win!

Sometimes you make choices that are clear cut and obvious. Others are well planned risks. Michele, without knowing it, had helped create what I call the "AFLAC® Miracle." I believe it was all a part of God's plan.

AFLAC® is the American Family Life Assurance Company of Columbus. Eight months before we knew about Kile's cancer, Michele had purchased a family policy from an AFLAC® representative. When I found out, I was upset. I objected to what I felt was unnecessary coverage. It was a cancer policy. As usual Michele did what she felt was best and kept the coverage. As much as you cannot place a dollar amount on pain and suffering, AFLAC® paid benefits in addition to and over and above our HMO insurance. Our agent's unheard of attention to detail and promptness helped us deal with the costs of travel, lodging and unexpected expenses. The remaining funds will also pay for his college education. Many families we met needed to hold bake sales and auctions to help pay for treatments let alone extra expenses. Some families lost everything.

In a letter to the main office of AFLAC® I told them, "AFLAC® didn't save my son's life, it gave him one!" Although he could not work, Kile continued to have spending money and wanted for nothing. In fact he was spoiled and deserved it. It was one battle we were winning . . . the fight for his dignity.

Whether you are fighting a disease or fighting for your dignity, the battle must be clearly understood and the fight is to the finish.

Having a game plan is half the battle. When was the last time you wrote down your goals? Never? If you don't know where you're going, how will you know when you have arrived? It takes no fancy forms or bookkeeping to have a plan. Grab a tablet and pencil (not an ink pen you'll need to make changes), and on one page write the heading "Today's Goals". Then continue with "This Week", "This Month", "This Year", "Five Years" and, yes, "Ten Years". Make your short-term goals specific. Break them down into small attainable goals that you know you can accomplish today. Each day should add to the next and then ultimately contribute to the bigger long-term goals. The Five and Ten-Year goals should be fun and bigger than life itself. They are the lofty dreams that are as attainable as the short-term goals but, in today's reality, out of reach.

At the end of each day, celebrate all that you have accomplished. Those items not finished are carried over to the next day or reconsidered. That's why you have written them in pencil, so you can make changes.

Don't quit! Reconstruct, redesign, but don't give up.

I know there are times when you'll want to. There will be times in your battle you'll just want to lay down and die. I know, I've been there.

8 ❖

The Casualties of War

This has been quite a year. Here I am nearly at the other end of Kile's treatment. He has been doing extremely well. His response to his therapy is excellent. They have removed the cancerous tumor along with a large part of the bone. We had feared for a short time that he might lose his leg. But they were able to replace that bone with a donor bone, insert a rod and several screws, and basically give Kile his life back.

During the period of Kile's treatment my career had been slowly coming to a halt. I hadn't noticed because I kept thanking God for providing the time I needed to be with my son. Had I been working a normal 9 to 5 job I would never have had the opportunity to stay over at the hospital.

Today I would not trade those hours for anything.

But as I was praising God for providing the opportunity, I was losing precious ground in business. The speaking industry is like any other business. In order to stay busy you need to stay on top of your marketing plan.

But for this past year I had had no plan.

I worked, and was able to pay bills, but I never took

time to plan for tomorrow. It was amazing that, no matter where my work took me, it never interfered with a scheduled hospital treatment. I figured it was all part of God's plan for me. But I failed to follow through on my end of the deal. My goal-setting plans fell apart.

You see, God does have a mission, a purpose for each of us. He does want us to trust in Him. But He also trusts in us to carry out the plan. You know right now, deep in your heart, that God has entrusted you with some incredible gifts and opportunities. But maybe you haven't acted on them. I'll bet many times you have complained about what's not right in your life while at the same time fighting off that burning desire placed in the deepest part of your soul by God Himself.

Maybe your poor self image has taken control of your life and you are no longer in charge. Perhaps you are convinced that you will never succeed at anything. Even if you are surrounded by things that success has bought you, you might still be unhappy because you are not heeding the call. There is a dream for each of us. Yours is not out of reach. It is within you—just below the surface of the armour you built to protect yourself from failure. Look at yourself. I dare you to stop right now and look in the mirror. Look beyond the surface. Stare into your eyes and ask yourself if you are all you would like to be. If the answer is "no," then face the fact that the only person stopping you is staring right back.

If you're feeling lousy about life right now, I know just how you feel. Because in the middle of all the excitement that Kile's recovery has brought to me I'm getting this unbelievable sinking feeling that I've been here before. As I look ahead for the next few months I have very few bookings. In fact in all of December and January there is nothing.

Now more than ever before I have a story to tell. I have seen the likes of failure. I have seen the face of a mother walking down the hallway of the hospital with her child. She was just told that morning that there is nothing more they can do. Tomorrow they go home and prepare for her child's death which may occur in a week, a month or in the next 24 hours.

I have also witnessed success. I have seen the joy of a family leaving after the last chemotherapy treatment. They fought and have won the battle this far. It's time now to celebrate. It's time for him to go back to school, grow up, fall in love, and have a family of his own.

But it's impossible to get anyone to understand how I feel now. They think they know how I should act and sound. When I'm down, my closest friends and family know it. But today even Kile's nurse sensed it when she stopped me in the hallway to ask me what was wrong.

I'm hurting and aching for people I don't even know. People who feel their lives are passing them by. Don't tell me this is unhealthy. Don't tell me to stop thinking this way. I can't and I won't. I've been right where they are and felt the same feelings. The hole that they have dug for themselves is deep and they're getting buried.

I want to share with them. I want to tell them what's happened in my life. I want to remind them how very important they are. I want to see what I call "The Look".

When I'm giving a speech and I shift into high gear, the audience can taste the passion I have for what I do. I scan across the crowd and there, right there on her face and his is "The Look." Their heads are cocked slightly to one side. The eyebrows are raised as if they are surprised to hear my message of hope. There's a sparkle, a glimmer in the eyes as the neck is stretched forward as if on the edge with anticipation. They look like children waiting for the next line in their favorite story. But these are adults wanting to hear me tell them how very important they are.

I can hear them say, "Tell me it's true. I do believe. Really I want to. But I'm not suppose to believe in dreams anymore. I've grown now." It pours right from their heart.

They are the first to stand up and applaud at the end. They do believe for now, for a while longer. Maybe even a week or two. Or at least until they go home to their spouses or friends who will try to bring them down to their level. "I ain't succeeding and neither will you!" they'll hear shortly.

Oh, the entire audience doesn't get it. Some are skeptics from the first word out of my mouth. Some get caught up in my message but dive right out the minute they start feeling good about themselves. The friend who came with them finds this all foolish. They might not appreciate their new found enthusiasm so they hold back. In many cases their spouse laughs at their attempts at personal improvement.

But they can't hide it from me. I see it. This is medicine for a dying dream. You can never breathe life into it with just one dose. Like my son's treatment, there's a protocol that you must follow. You can't stop half way through it just because you feel better today. Your attitude change needs the full prescription, or this dream will die for sure.

Believe it or not, I have the solution but I've failed on my end to get the message through. I thought I did all the right things. If God really wanted me to take all this experience I have and share it, doors would have opened wide. But by the looks of my schedule I've failed again.

Maybe the plan was just to get me through this until Kile's ordeal was over and I would then need to return to a new career. But I can't. I won't. I'm done starting over. I can't take this roller-coaster ride any more. Either God will open another door or I will close one . . . on my life.

How could this all happen to me again? Six years ago my world fell apart and now it has again.

This is just about where this story started. But now I am 46 years old and faced with another failed opportunity. I am exhausted from the fight for my son. Thoughts of giving up on all of my plans and returning to a normal 9 to 5 job are unbearable. Why would God give me these gifts and then take them all away? I have learned so much in these past six years from all of the personal experiences I've had. These stories are repeated in lives all around this great country. I know how they feel. I thought I was reaching so many of them. Or was I? Could I possibly measure one successful life that resulted from my efforts? If all that I told them was true, then why am I a failure again? Why did it all have to stop?

I was about to find out. I simply needed a reminder, just like you do. Someone needed to tell me how very important I am. I was about to discover that I am the most important person in the world. My world. And I would be, *"ever more"*.

9 ❖

One Last Word

*I*t seems to me that all I can be is whatever I make my mind up to be. Is it a
problem for me to understand that?
Can I possibly grow beyond this level I have reached? Or
am I doomed for eternity? It's a question I needed to answer and a problem I needed to solve . . . right now.

It appears, at least on the surface to be a simple
enough thing to do. Because more than half the battle in
trying to "arrive" is in deciding to "go." As I mentioned
earlier, the link between deciding where you want to go
and arriving is the plan you develop on how you'll get
there.

The first road block to overcome is to not just sit there
dreaming, but to take action steps toward your dreams.
For some of us our lives are always in the planning stages.
In the beginning, these grandiose dreams grab the attention of many friends and may be even one of the reasons
your spouse or mate found you exciting. You had big
plans. If you have been in the planning stages for a long
period of time, you've probably noticed that many of
those who believed in you years ago have fallen to the
side lines. Those who truly love you have hung in and,
because of their commitment to you, have helped keep
the embers glowing in the fire that once was a bright
burning flame.

You have probably gotten caught up in the lie yourself because you've talked about "some day" and "tomorrow" so long that you have become your greatest cheerleader instead of actually being on the field of play. So who's taking action on your dream?

No one.

I know, because I am the one who killed my dream and I was about to bury it.

Kile's last treatment would soon take place. There would be a grand celebration with music and family and friends. I would have no reason to miss this final trip to the clinic, because I had no work scheduled for the rest of this year. Which also means I'd once again have little money to make Christmas special for my family. But they have come to accept that because it had been that way for much too long.

My plan was to be there when they disconnected Kile for the last time. I wanted to watch the last drop of this medicine go through the tubing, say a prayer of thanks to God for saving his life, and say my good-byes.

I couldn't face the fact that my situation would require me to go back into the work force doing something I hated to do, working for someone else and getting caught up in the rat race that most of the world faced each day. How would I face family and friends when I had to admit that once again my dreams had failed.

I couldn't start over again in a few months. I had my chance at making my dreams work and I failed. The only good thing I did this past year was to be there for Kile. I wanted to go out with at least one success. Of course I know that Michele deserved better. She had been so incredible through all of my ups and downs and I had not made it easy for her. Many times I would place the blame for my failure on her. As if it was all her fault. Losers do that. It's always someone else's fault, or your circumstances that are the real reason why you're not happy. Losers never face the facts; they only distort them.

At this point I felt there was only one logical thing to do. Exactly what many other losers would consider. I would end my life right after Kile's treatment.

One week before his last hospital visit I received a call from a woman who had gotten my name through an associate. The phone rang late that night. It startled me.

"Hello. Is this Christian Tyler? I'm sorry for calling at this late hour. My name is Monica Snyder and I'm hoping you can help me."

She explained that a speaker originally scheduled to talk at a conference the following week had had to cancel. She was in charge of the presenters and had been desperately trying to fill the spot.

"Mr. Tyler, I have contacted everyone on my list. At this late date they are either booked or just unavailable. This keynote address is the focal point of the entire conference. We have members and their families coming from around the world. You can imagine the predicament that I'm in."

"Yes, Ms. Snyder, I can. But it seems to me that the speaker you are looking for would need to be a headliner. Someone who could really get the message across," I said.

"You're right, but do you know how difficult . . ."

I interrupted her: "I know how difficult it is to get the big names booked. But if it's a big name you are looking for why would you call me? Are you that desperate?"

"Mr. Tyler, I realize that you may not have the professional experience I'm looking for. But your name was mentioned to me by nearly everyone who had turned me down. You have exactly what I need in personal experience.".

"Look, I really appreciate your call but things have been very difficult for us lately . . . "

"Permit me to interrupt you, Mr. Tyler. That's exactly why we need you. It's because of your personal difficulties. Only a person who has experienced cancer in his family could speak from the heart at this conference," she said.

"Who are these people anyway?" I asked.

"*Families Can Survive.* They are families of cancer victims and survivors. We can all understand the obvious pain and grief families experience when someone is lost to cancer. But there is also the trauma of living the rest of your life after a loved one has survived cancer. The cancer patients and those who love them always live on the edge. As years pass they must learn to live with cancer even though at a measured point they are told their cancer is in remission or they are cancer-free. We still don't know enough about the disease to understand why, with some people, it returns even after they've been free of it for decades."

"We have a generous sponsor who is willing to pay $10,000 for your participation and, of course, whatever travel expenses you may incur."

"Ms. Snyder, that's more than double my normal fee." I said.

"It may be. But he insists that if we can get you he will pay the $10,000 and make a sizeable contribution to cancer research." she said.

"Who is he?" I asked.

"I'm sorry. He wishes to remain anonymous," she said.

"Can I have until morning to give you an answer?" I asked.

"I guess I can wait, Mr. Tyler. It's really too late to reach anyone else. But, I really don't think you're going to turn this one down."

Michele had heard bits and pieces of my conversation and was very curious as to what it was all about. I explained, and told her I had until morning to decide.

"Christian, what's there to decide?" she asked as we got ready for bed. "You have been anxious to get back to work and what better group to speak to after all this time off than to people you can personally relate to. Once they hear your insight on this, it will make a world of difference to them."

"I don't know if I have it in me, Michelle. It has been much too long. I've lost again. I'm right back to where I was before. Our bills are behind. The car payment and the mortgage are at least three months late," I said. "Christmas is coming and we need things for the house. And what about your car, Michele? You have over 150,000 miles on it."

I knew that the money would help pay many of the bills. But I was tired, defeated and feared that it would be even more difficult to let go . . . of my dreams, my family and my life.

"How much would we need to get your business going again?" she asked.

"Don't even think about it, Michele. With all my debt, and the money I would need just to do a proper marketing piece, you're probably talking about $10,000, and that would . . ." I stopped for a moment and thought about what I just said. $10,000. That's exactly what they wanted to pay me.

"That would what?" Michele asked. "What were you going to say?"

I hadn't told Michele how much they offered me. "That would . . . be fine if this speaking engagement paid anything. They offered just to pay my expenses because they are a non-profit" I told her. "Let's go to sleep. We will talk about it in the morning."

The night dragged on like so many nights had in this past year. I couldn't sleep thinking about this offer. Maybe I would do this one last speech. I could ask them to send the check in Michele's name to my home address. This might just work out fine. After giving the talk I could slip back to the hotel. I'd make some excuse to Michele for not inviting her along. I had enough valium and sleeping pills collected in the past year to do the job. I'd be out of town and my family wouldn't have to be the ones to find my body.

One last speech. Between the check and insurance money I could leave her debt-free. I had also fulfilled my commitment to Kile. I was there every step of the way throughout his recovery. As for my youngest son Kevin, I knew he'd do just fine. He had been a fortress throughout this past year. With all of the attention Kile had received Kevin never once complained. He's a marvelous wit, and incredibly creative. I'm proud to have him call me Dad. Both of my sons are my greatest contribution to this world.

The next day I called Ms. Snyder to confirm the engagement. I gave her all of the specifics, and she insisted on making my travel plans.

Everything was to be arranged by an agent from *Amore Travel*, including first class seating and full escort at any terminal transfer. Of course a limo at the airport. *Amore* Travel "Love." What a way to go.

10 ❖

The Sky is the Limit

You would think that I would have learned some hard lessons from that experience six years ago. You would think that having the taste of failure so fresh on my mind, I would never fall into that same rut again.

But here I am once more. Lessons learned, life lived, yet disaster is waiting nearby like a thief in darkness, ready to steal everything I value. But I did give it a try. I risked all I had, and then some. Here I am freshly scarred from the battle, wounded almost fatally this time. Down and I don't want to get up.

I have decided, just like a loser would, to run away from it all. Acting like a child who doesn't get his way, I want to quit. I don't want to be a part of life. Alone in a world filled with people. It sounds like an impossible task. But if one chooses, one can be alone in a crowded elevator. Alone is a box you create in your mind. It's an island in the grey matter where your day begins and ends. Alone is a temporary stop or a sadly permanent destination. But like everything in life it's a choice. Your choice.

I can't stand the idea of returning to life the way it was before. I was supposed to accomplish big things this time. But I screwed up, as I always did before. I'm too old to start over again. I just can't face my family and friends as a failure. By now I must be a joke in their eyes. What have I done for them? In what way have I contributed to a better life for my children? Michele was the only responsible one in this marriage. By now she must be tired of all the promises I've made. Year after year I've talked to her of better times ahead. I've spoken of a bigger home and nicer clothes and a lifestyle she deserved so much.

I could go home and find a real job and slip slowly back into obscurity. But I couldn't stand it. I'd be miserable, and I'd make everyone's life a living hell. I love them all so very much. But I can't stand this pain. I have spent days on end wallowing in my tears. There is an ache in my body that screams to me: "Do something!" I've drowned out that voice of possibilities and smothered it with negativity. I don't want to hear what I should do. I've listened to that voice before and made a fool of myself, dragging everyone around me down to the deepest depths of despair. My body hurts. My mind is tired of plotting and planning. I just want desperately to stop.

There is only one possible answer. I know without a doubt in my mind that their lives would be better without me. I do have a choice. I've chosen the fool's way out. I'll end my life right after my final speech.

Have you ever thought about what it would be like if you knew when you were going to die and you could make all of the final arrangements the day before? That's what it's been like for me every time I take a long trip. The day before I have always made sure I've left the proper notes for everyone. I realize now that I always lived in fear. But not today.

Today I will enjoy my time, spending it with people I love. I called my father last night and asked him out for breakfast. You always need to ask him the night before. It's not that he has a lot of plans, he just has routine, a pattern that his everyday life follows.

Dad and I agreed to meet at the restaurant at 10:00 a.m. That means he'll be there 15–20 minutes before that. I've learned to work it into my plans when I'm with him. If not, the first words out of his mouth are "I've been waiting here for 15 minutes." I've given up trying to explain that *I'm* on time *he's* early. Since he's been back in my life I have learned it's easier not to argue with him. There's just no sense in it. You're wasting your breath and his.

He's a good man and has worked hard all of his life. He's had a tough time from childhood until now focusing on the positive. He had a difficult childhood and it shows. I've always had a healthy respect for his authority when I was growing up. In fact it bordered on fear. All my mother needed to say to me when I misbehaved was: "Wait until your father gets home!" Those words and the sound of his footsteps were torture enough. He was a mechanic, and after a tough day the last thing he wanted to hear when he walked in the door was that I had done something wrong.

He isn't physically a big man but when I was a child he was enormous in my eyes. But not now. Not today. He's 80 this year. Shorter than I remember him, and a great deal slower. One day, after moving into his apartment after the divorce from his second wife, he suddenly realized how dependent he had become. He cried and reached out for me as I was leaving. He hugged me and laid his head on my chest. It reminded me of a children's fairy tale when the big monster is slain and the characters stand around it looking down at it with sadness in their hearts even though it brought fear into their lives.

When I look at him I always remember that song called *"The leader of the band."* One line goes . . . "The leader of the band is tired and his eyes are growing old. But his blood runs through my instrument and his song is in my soul." The writer later refers to his father's "thundering velvet hand." That was the one thing about my

Pop. I can say he really left an impression on me. Literally.

Breakfast goes fine. We have our usual conversation about why his wife left him. He says he doesn't understand. I think he does. But we discuss it anyway.

We say our good-byes in the parking lot. I sit an extra minute to see him drive away. Maybe for the last time. His or mine. Then there it is again. That same message I've heard too many times now, quietly, softly whispering in my ear what sounds like *"Ever more"* I still don't understand what it means. But I always hear it right after a critical moment in my life. It's like a reassurance.

Upon returning home I check my phone for messages. I haven't heard from anyone in weeks. But there is one message from the travel agent. "There's been a change in your flight plans to Wisconsin for the conference. Everything is right on schedule, but I had to switch airlines for one portion of your trip. You will now be flying on "Celestial Air" out of Pittsburgh to Cleveland, and then back to US Air onto LaCrosse. Your tickets will be waiting at your first connection."

I needed to pick up a few things before day's end so I headed to a local department store where I ran into my brother and sister-in-law. I wanted to speak to them anyway so this made it even more convenient. They were there because they, too, needed a few things for a trip they were taking. In recent years they have been taking more time to do things for themselves. Their three children are grown and on their own. My sister-in-law retired early, so she's been developing her talents waiting for the day he'll quit work. They were headed for an overnight bus trip. I never saw them happier. They deserve these moments. They were aware of my last minute plans and wished me a safe trip. We said our good-byes and, as they headed for the checkout area, he stopped, turned, and smiled at me. My mind flashed back to just a few weeks ago when I had held their first grandchild. Tears had run down my face as I looked at this beautiful baby. I held the future. He was an extension of us.

I waved good-bye and went about my shopping. I was to meet my youngest son right after school. We often head to this great ice cream and sandwich shop near his house. At around 3:00 p.m. it's quiet there, and we can have a great conversation. He always makes me laugh, and I needed that from him today more than ever. He didn't let me down. We laughed about the silliest things and, before we knew it, our time had run out.

We had made a pact in recent years. Every time we said our prayers, no matter where we were, we would ask God to keep us together. I always feared that his mom and step dad would move away. All I ever asked of God was for me to be with him until he graduated from high school. I know he will probably leave home for college, so it wasn't much to ask God for a mere seven more years. But now it didn't make any difference. I was leaving for good.

Just before he got out of the car he said, "I'll say a prayer as usual for a safe trip. Should I still keep praying for that miracle, Dad?" "Yes, Kevin. I could use one right now," I said. "I love you. Get a hundred. Remember that no matter what happens, I'll always love you."

As I drove away I could see him in my rear view mirror, running on the sidewalk, racing me.

Then suddenly he stopped and broke into this crazy dance he does. I could see him as he signed, "I love You," to me one last time.

"Ever more" There it was again. Should I have expected anything else? I've become comfortable with hearing it now. But I'd sure like to understand why me?

I drove to the store near my home. I had planned a special meal for us. No sooner had I walked into the market when I met Jason and Gabrielle. They're friends from a long time ago. Both have become part-time ministers in a small church they founded. Gabrielle has a special gift from God. She senses things just from a conversation she has with you. Not always. But there have been some incredible insights in the past. It's almost mystical.

She told me once that God was calling me for a purpose and he wouldn't wait much longer for me to follow. It was shortly after that I got into the speaking business. I swore this was it. I really believed that this career was part of God's plan for me. It all seemed so perfectly clear. I guess I was wrong.

We hugged and talked for a while. Jason excused himself to grab a spot in the deli line. I was a bit nervous because Gabrielle had that look in her eye. I was afraid to hear what she had to say.

"You've answered the call, Christian, haven't you?" she said. "He's waiting again. There's something you have to do before the full plan can be revealed."

I couldn't believe I was hearing this. I was so tired of waiting. I was so sick of just getting by.

"Gabrielle, I've done everything I can. There's nothing left in me. I've prayed and listened and knocked on too many doors. It's over," I said.

"Your dreams and hopes will take flight very soon. Keep believing," she said as Jason returned.

"Christian, I'll pray for you tonight. My heart tells me your answers are in the heavens. You have a lesson to learn. Your happiness will be *ever more*." They turned and walked away.

"*Ever more*." There it was. She said it this time. "Your happiness will be *ever more*"

I don't even know about *tomorrow* let alone *ever more*. My answers are in the heavens, she said. We'll see. I already feel relieved in my decision to end it all. I want to enjoy this final trip but I'm hurting so very much today. Maybe tomorrow. I've always lived for tomorrow.

11 ❖

Celestial Intervention

5:00 a.m. should be against the law. Let's form a committee, start a congressional investigation, and then a support group. No one should get up this early.

"Yesterday is history. Tomorrow is a mystery. Today is a gift. That's why we call it the present." A woman in Texas walked up and handed me that message right after I finished speaking to the Texas Credit Union League a few years ago. I never forgot it. Today it popped in my mind immediately after my cursing the alarm clock radio.

When Michele and I get up this early we usually have very little to say. We seem to sleepwalk right until that first cup of coffee, even though most of the time it's decaf. You don't need caffeine in your life to get you going. You need motivation from within, and a healthy life style.

Our plan was to be at the airport one hour before departure. So far everything was running right on time. We even found an open parking spot right in front of the door. The line for check-in was short, and we got a great table in the coffee shop overlooking the runway. We had less than an hour together for breakfast. We went over some last minute details and, as always, I promised to call as soon as I arrived at the hotel.

This is always the most difficult part for me. Our good-byes. But this was even more difficult. If all went the way I planned, this truly would be our last good-bye. Standing just outside the security entrance I looked into her eyes, wanting to say so much to her. Like, thanks for always permitting me to dream. Thanks for picking up the tab for debts I made in pursuit of that dream.

"Thanks for loving me," I said softly. We kissed as our eyes filled with "I'll-miss-you" tears. I turned and crossed through security and, looking back, I signed "I Love you," just as Kevin and I did just last night. It's a ritual my son Kile and I started, and finished much too soon.

There Michele and I stood on each side of a glass partition. What torture for me. I wanted to hold her until the last second. I needed to walk away feeling the warmth of her body burned in my memory. Just as they announced boarding I turned one last time, tears now running down my cheeks. Find someone who can give you all that you deserve, Michele. I'm a loser and you've lost too much already. Go ahead now, enjoy life. Remember me as a dreamer who only wanted the best, but failed trying. I quietly whispered, "I Love you". She replied, "I love you too," turned, and walked away.

I suppose the plane could have been smaller. But not much. I always request aisle seats rather than window for all of my trips. On this small plane it didn't make a difference. This was a 19 seater Beechcraft 1900D. It almost looked new. The windows were big oval portals, and you could actually stand up once you boarded the plane. I've had to walk on smaller planes slumped over.

There were no bathrooms, nor were there any bright and chipper flight attendants greeting us. In fact, there was a recorded message to give us the run-through about exits and seatbelts. As I sat in the plane looking out the window, I could see Michele behind a tall fence on the observation deck on top of the building. It was much too cold for her to be out there. I waved frantically, but to no avail. She couldn't see me. But I had a chance for one last look at the woman I loved so much.

Checking my tickets I noted my connection in Pittsburgh was pretty tight. I was to board Celestial Air, Flight #22. As smoothly as everything was going today even the flight number gave me added comfort. You see "2" is my favorite number. It reminds me of the second chance I had in life, my second wife, and my two sons. In fact the day I got married to Michele our room by chance was 222. Lucky? Obviously not, if you look at my life today. But there is no such thing as luck. Luck is when opportunity meets preparedness. Obviously I wasn't prepared.

I always loved traveling to new cities, meeting new people and sharing stories with them. This trip would be a challenge for me. Part of me, this small spark deep inside my heart, was anxious to get there. The rest was dreading the moment. What was I going to say to this group? How could I stand there and tell them how wonderful life was and how bright their future could be if only they would trust in the God who created them. I had given up. Fear took over faith. A friend had recently told me that fear is the faith of the Devil. Faith is only faith when you can't see. You learn to trust that all will work out for the good. This speech would need to be more of a performance, requiring my best acting abilities to get a positive message across.

Actor. Charmer. Both words were often used to describe me by my teachers in grade school. My parents would return from a PTA meeting after hearing, "Christian is a fine boy. Although he struggles to keep even average grades, he's a real charmer in class." It was their only hope for me.

This short trip to Pittsburgh was nearly over. Looking out the window the view was all too familiar. I had taken this trip many times before. The land, the foggy rivers, looked much like home. But there, jutting out of the mist, were the big city monuments to capitalism. The point where three rivers met the Steelers and Pirates. People scrambled below to get to work and day care, and some, were just going home after working night shift somewhere.

My destination was Wisconsin. All I needed to do was find my connection. Celestial Air. I had never heard of it. One of the pilots made announcements for flight connections but never mentioned this airline. "Oh, it's going to be one of those days," I said out loud.

Upon arrival, as we entered the terminal, I asked an attendant where flight 22 Celestial Air would be departing.

"Pardon me?" he asked. "US Air?"

"No. Celestial Air flight #22," I repeated.

"Sorry sir, I have no listing for . . . "

"Mr. Tyler, Mr. Tyler!" a voice cried out. There, just to my right, was a young lady. Her warm welcoming smile gave me comfort immediately.

"Yes, I'm Christian Tyler."

"I know," she said. "I'm Jennifer Harris. Please follow me."

"You know I'm running late. I'm trying to catch my next flight to Cleveland. No one seems to know anything about the airline Celestial Air. Can you help me?" I asked.

"Relax, Mr. Tyler." she said. "The plane is waiting for you. Here have a seat."

She pointed to an airport shuttle cart. I couldn't believe it. I've seen these carts zooming through airports and always wanted to ride one. The people look so important. "Move out of the way!" it seems to shout. "We're going places!"

"Please sit here, Mr. Tyler. We'll be at the gate in a few minutes," said Jennifer.

The ride was smooth. Everything I thought it would be. We rolled down the all-too-familiar concourse, past the small shops and news stands. There, on my left, was Bains Deli. It's my favorite sandwich stop on layovers in Pittsburgh.

"You won't need to stop here for a turkey sandwich today, Mr. Tyler," Jennifer said softly.

"Turkey? That's my favorite sandwich."

"Yes, I know. Heavy on the mayo, Italian bread, and, of course, cranberry sauce on top. Whole berry, not jellied," she said.

"Why yes, " I said, surprised. "But how would you know that?"

"You'll have a fine meal in flight, Mr. Tyler. We're here. Please go through that door and to your right. Your flight is waiting." She never answered my question. Perhaps it's a popular sandwich here in Pittsburgh. I had never had one until I met Michele.

I was on a concourse with very few people. Normally an attendant would take my ticket before reaching the plane. But I was running late and this was a small airline.

There standing at the door to the plane was a very distinguished looking gray haired man wearing a navy blue suit and bright-colored tie. He had the same comforting smile as Jennifer.

"Oh, Mr. Tyler. We've been waiting," he said. "Welcome to Celestial Air."

It was odd to me that both he and Jennifer knew my name. Perhaps from the boarding list, I thought.

"Celestial Air, yes. I was concerned that I wouldn't find you. No one seemed to know what I was talking about."

"We are a small private airline. Our clientele are referred to us through an exclusive system. By the way I'm Mr. More," he said, handing me his business card. "A. More" it read. No fancy print or company logo. And no mention of Celestial Air.

"A. More as in Amore Travel?" I asked.

"Yes." he replied.

"But there's no title here. Are you the owner?" I asked.

"Yes, you could say that," he said with a chuckle. "My unofficial title is 'Scavenger.'"

"Scavenger?" I repeated. "How odd. A friend once called me a scavenger live on the air during my radio show I had at the time."

"How did it make you feel?" he asked.

"Honored," I replied. "It's exactly what I was. She told me I rummaged through life finding lost treasures, people the world never took notice of. She was right."

"Why do you speak in the past tense, Mr. Tyler? You're still scavenging, aren't you?"

"Not after this week, I'm sorry to say."

"I think this trip will change all of that," said Mr. More.

"Amore. That means love doesn't it? It's quite unusual," I said.

"Yes, Mr. Tyler it is. But so is being a scavenger."

"Well, I had better be seated. I'm holding everyone up," I said.

"We have plenty of time. Please, sit right here."

I hadn't noticed until now that my seat was first class. In fact the entire plane was first class. There were large soft seats, with plenty of room to stretch out. I was right up front. Now I knew why they called it Celestial Air. This was heavenly.

Before long we were airborne. They offered me all of the amenities, including a warm wash cloth to refresh my face. Wine, champagne, or anything else I wanted, was available to drink. I couldn't believe it. What a way to go out. My last speech, and first class all the way.

"Mr. Tyler. I do hope you're hungry," said Mr. More as he placed my meal on the tray in front of me.

It was a huge, freshly sliced turkey sandwich with all the trimmings. Exactly the way I liked it.

It was about 45 minutes into the flight when Mr. More approached me. "May I join you?" he asked.

"Yes, please do."

His card lay on the tray next to a tablet where I was trying desperately to write the speech I was to give that evening.

"What's the "A" stand for Mr. More?" I asked.

"Avery, Avery More," he replied.

There was something familiar about the sound of his voice. Even that name. Was that the voice I'd been hearing? *"Ever more,"* I whispered softly.

"No, Avery More," he said.

"Yes, Yes. I'm sorry. It's just that . . . never mind."

"Having trouble with the speech? I wouldn't worry. You'll know exactly what to say when the time comes."

"How did you know that I was writing a speech, Avery?"

"I can see that you are a businessman. Presentations are a part of life in business."

"Yes, but this is a very significant speech. It's my last one."

"Mr. Tyler, you give up too soon."

"Please Avery, call me Christian," I insisted.

"Christian, this is only the beginning for you. You cannot begin to imagine what lies ahead. It's even more important than what you have accomplished so far. You are an important man."

Avery and I talked for what seemed like hours. We were both so in tune with each other. I could see in his eyes, the passion he had for life. The love he had for people was obvious. It was the best conversation I had had in years.

"Avery, this is all great. But the fact is I have failed. I've failed in my attempt to get this message out. I have done all that I can to reach people. But I've not made one measurable difference. I *have* failed," I said.

"Christian, I refuse to settle for that kind of thinking. I know that deep inside, you don't really believe it. Will you agree that it is impossible for any living soul to go from birth to death without influencing others around them? Our everyday living and breathing, working and playing, serves as an example to dozens of people who cross our paths." Avery began to sound upset.

"Yes, I agree. From the next door neighbor to the grocery clerk at the store, we can't help but leave an impression on those we come in contact with. But I am speaking of a real *influence*. A measurable change in someone's life that occurred because of an action I've taken, one speech I've given."

"Christian, here's solid proof," he said with a sparkle in his eye. "Three years ago you began a radio program on a small AM station in your area. You called it the "Success Connection."

"Yes, but how would you . . . "

"Wait. Permit me to finish." he interrupted. "It was difficult in the beginning. You were never sure how many people were listening. Your community wasn't ready for this type of programming. One woman named Susan had lost everything. Gradually, through the years, she had permitted everyone around her to control her destiny. She looked to them for everything. She lost her self respect. She really felt she had nothing to offer life. Gradually she confined herself to the small world in which she lived. She never left her building."

"How typical that is of so many people," Christian said.

"Yes. But then one day, while flipping through the radio channels, she heard your voice and your familiar phrase: 'I believe in you!' Never before in her meager life had she heard those words. That was two-and-a-half years ago. Today she is out in the community nearly every day. Her involvement in church and social activities has brought new life to a dull existence. She has discovered her full potential for life."

"Maybe so, Avery. But it wasn't due to me. I always told my audience that I stand on the shoulders of giants.

I researched and studied the greats in history such as Lincoln, Churchill, and Roosevelt. And, of course, our modern-day masters like Robert H. Schuller, Og Mandino, Norman Vincent Peale, and Dr. Wayne Dyer. It's not the messenger. It's the message."

"But it *is* the messenger too, Christian. For example, you have influenced scores of people such as Susan who, from a distance, have seen how you live. Did your actions match your message?" he retorted.

"But she didn't know me," I said.

"Yes, Christian, she did. That's her, fifth row on the right. Look at her. A perfect picture of happiness."

"That's her? How do you know that's her? What is she doing on this flight?"

Avery sat quietly for a moment. He shifted about in his seat, glancing past me out the window. Then, turning his head toward me he smiled and said, "I just do, Christian."

There was something in his words, his smile, that satisfied my curiosity. I didn't press forward with my questioning. For some reason I trusted Avery.

"Christian," he said. "You have come to a special place in your life. You have approached this crossroad on your path as if it were a dead end. In reality it's a transition. You are about to soar to new heights in your career. Yet you have failed to see the significance of all the losses you have felt and journeys you have taken along the way to arrive at this point."

"Oh, please don't tell me that God permitted all of these troubles and disappointments so I could share my experience with others. I accepted that for a time, Avery. But then it just began to seem like a string of bad luck," I said.

"There's no such thing as luck, Christian."

"I know, I know. I've said that to audiences a hundred times. Luck is when opportunity meets preparedness. Well, I guess I was prepared for bad things to happen."

"Yes, you were. Your faith, your survival instincts, your compassion for others, prepared you to get through it all to discover your mission, your purpose in life."

It all sounded wonderful coming from Avery. But look at where I was today. Not another booking in the new year, no inquiries, nothing.

"Beyond that lady there in the fifth row I've failed to make any measurable difference during my six years in this business, let alone in my life."

"Not so, Christian. Along the way you have taken it upon yourself to do many special things for friends as well as perfect strangers. The notes left for waitresses, the special words face to face with a clerk or bell hop. The flower you handed to a young lady on the square during the festival back home."

"She looked like she needed it, Avery. That look on her face. She looked lonely and sad. I had to do something." I said.

"You're right, Christian. She had just lost her mother the week before. They had always attended that festival together. It was a tradition filled with many wonderful memories for her. That's her in the sixth row."

"Now wait a minute. What's going on here? I could accept the possibility that the first woman might be on this plane. But another? And how would you know about this?" I asked. "This conversation will end right now if I don't get an explanation."

"You're right. It is time for an explanation. But I ask you to listen first to what I have to say. I'll be happy to answer any questions you may have afterwards."

I wasn't really sure if I was ready to hear this. I wanted to know, yet this was just a little too much for me. Avery was about to reveal a most incredible story. A system designed by God to keep us on the path.

12 ❖

My God!
I did All That?

We now must have been in flight for nearly five hours. I had completely lost track of where we should have been by now. The flight to Cleveland should have been about an hour. I was either very late or very lost.

"Do you believe that every human being has a purpose, a mission in life?" asked Avery.

"Yes. In fact my career was based on that very principle," I replied.

"My purpose is to seek out the guided ones. We call them *Connectors*. Every human being was given a gift at birth. It is the gift of *choice*. You have shared this concept with every audience you have spoken to. But it wasn't until recently that you really understood. Nothing controls us. But there is a small voice inside each of us. Some call it intuition. Many are comfortable with calling on that voice for direction. Others, however, fight it all the way. They overpower that voice with their own thoughts of negativity. It's what holds them back and even destroys their lives. Connectors are special individuals who have been placed on this earth as guides. God uses these special people to encourage, motivate, inspire others whose mission is of great importance. They are like traffic cops keeping people's spirits on the right path."

"Are these Connectors all leaders?" I asked.

"No, Christian, they are not. Many are everyday people dispersed throughout life, working side by side with their neighbors and friends. They are there right in your community."

"This sounds too much like an Isaac Asminov science fiction story," I said.

"No, more like the inspiration of Og Mandino or Robert H. Schuller," said Avery.

"Mr. Mandino is dead. What an incredible loss to the world."

"There is no loss when your purpose has been fulfilled," said Avery. "Mr. Mandino has left a legacy that will live forever. His writings and recorded messages will outlive us all. He will continue to positively affect the world for eternity."

"I loved that man but I never got the chance to meet him," said Christian. "I wanted so much to tell him how important he was."

"But you did. When you wrote to him just a few months before he died, you sent him your tape and two 'I Believe in You' T-shirts. One for him and one for his wife, Bette."

"I never expected him to write back, but he did. I still have his handwritten message at home. I was so excited. I had read his book 'The Spellbinder's Gift', the story of a very special speaker who had a very important message for the world. He was discovered by an agent who, after trying retirement for a year, found that his mission was not yet complete. I wrote to Og in search of an agent just like that. I'll never forget the line he wrote to me. 'I never recommend speakers to my agent but contact her and mention my name.'" Christian took a deep breath and paused for a moment.

"He believed in your message, Christian."

"But I never could get his agent to understand," said Christian.

"It wasn't the right time. But she was the right agent."

"Did Og really believe in my message?"

"Christian, he gave one shirt to Bette as requested. The other he gave to a friend he believed in. In fact, to this day, during warm weather in New Hampshire, that shirt can be seen around his home town. Can you imagine how important it is to the recipient now that Og is gone? You have helped people you haven't even met."

"Do you mean to tell me that Og was a Connector, too?"

"Yes. And like you he needed to be in the public eye. There are those Connectors who need to reach the masses through their writing and speaking. Others are in leadership roles in business and government. Many lead ordinary lives but have the extraordinary ability to inspire others by their actions and encouraging words."

"Since everyone in life has a purpose, a mission, the Connectors help them to fulfill those tasks. We are all very important and play a significant part in the advancement of the human spirit. There is no one person more important than the other."

"And you? What part do you play in all of this?" I asked. "I suppose that you are an angel of some sort."

"Oh, I guess you can say that. I like the word scavenger better. I search out the lost and misguided Connectors. 'Celestial Air' is the flight of a lifetime. I guess you can say these are my wings," he said, pointing out the window.

"What about the rest of these people on the plane. Who are they?"

"They are just some of the people you have influenced in your life. And a few you haven't met yet. But you will."

"Who is that older gentlemen in the back of the plane? He looks familiar to me," I asked.

"He should. You shared an apple with him almost daily."

"The bus driver from the retirement home! I remember I met him when I worked there. He drove the bus on my avenue when I was a child. When I worked at the retirement center I would stop in his room almost daily and he'd cut up an apple as we talked about the good old days," I said.

"He always looked forward to that. He cried the day you told him you were leaving."

"Yes, he did. I remember I felt so bad," I said. "How's that a good thing, Avery? I walked out on him ."

"You made his last few days very special. He died the next day."

I sat quietly. I was at a loss for words. I gazed out the window at the houses below.

"What about all of them? There are so many people wandering through life aimlessly. They've lost faith in themselves, in their country and, worse yet, God."

"That's why we have Connectors there too. They're everyday people who, just by the way they live and work, influence the ones around them."

"Avery, what about the children? Where does this all begin?" asked Christian.

"Well, Connectors are born not made. They are destined from birth to negotiate, to take the role of mediator. Among their peers they rarely take sides and tend to get along with anyone. You were that way, Christian."

"I guess I was. Whatever I had, I shared. I had the respect of the little guy and the bully."

"You also touched lives back then. Do you remember the man in the abandoned railroad building?"

"Why yes, I do. My 'I Believe in You Bracelet' was designed after the leather and beads he left for me."

"Your efforts that day saved that man's life. It wasn't just the Kool Aid® and cookies, it was your act of kindness. It gave him hope. Everyone had been turning their backs on him for days. He wandered from town to town living out of garbage cans. His life was over, Christian. He crawled into that building to die. Your gesture of love was not only nourishment for the body but strength for his soul. He was able to get to a local shelter, and from there, with a little financial help from the Salvation Army, back to his family. He went on with life as a family man and a successful minister."

"Is he here, on the plane?" Christian stood and turned back toward the other passengers.

"Yes, Christian, he is." Avery reached into his pocket, opened his hand, and there was the 1943 Liberty half dollar.

"No, my God. It isn't you." Christian slowly turned the coin over and there under the left wing of the eagle was the heart etched by his grandfather.

"I have kept this coin all of my life. You told me it was lucky. But things don't possess luck; people possess the ability to love and be loved. That is truly all we need," said Avery. "My mouth was dry and swollen from malnourishment. You kept asking my name and I kept telling you *"Avery More."* But all you could hear was *"Ever More"*.

"I had forgotten about that until a few years ago. Then I began hearing the voice. Your voice?" Christian asked.

"Yes, Christian. Upon completion of my mission here on earth, I was assigned to watch over certain Connectors whose lives needed direction. You were one of them. Every time you found yourself in a difficult situation I tried desperately to jog your memory back to that day you helped me. I did it by repeating *"Ever more,"* as you understood it to be. I wanted you to know how important you were and how much you were still needed."

"That's what I've been telling people at my speaking engagements, Avery. Everyone plays an important part in life. Each one touches another through a smile, a kind word, or caring actions. The woman down the street from where I live plants the most incredible flower garden in her front yard. No one knows a thing about her. She never speaks a word. But her efforts, her flowers, brighten the neighborhood and bring joy to anyone driving by. Oh, Avery, I've tried to get through to them, but they have been conditioned to believe that success is measured by the clothes you wear, who you know, and the size of your bank account."

"We both know how wrong that is," he said. I could hear the passion in his voice. "You have a big job ahead. You need to get focused. We're depending on you."

"But Avery, how focused can I be when my son . . . my own son has cancer." Even to this day when I say that word it's like hearing it for the first time. "Was that a lesson, too?" I asked angrily. "Did my son get cancer so I could have more material for my speeches?" I realized how very stupid it sounded even before I finished.

"If that were so, what use is that young child's cancer?" he asked, pointing to a young couple seated on the left, halfway back.

The child was around eight years old. He was laughing and bouncing around like any other eight year old. The only difference was he was bald. The baseball cap he wore could barely cover the obvious.

"Have I met them too? Are they a part of all this?" I asked.

"Everyone here is. But, no, you haven't met the Phillipses. You will. The next time you go to Hershey for your son's scheduled check up they will be there. This young boy has a brain tumor."

"I never know what to say to parents whose child has cancer," I said.

"What did everyone say to you?" asked Avery.

"Be positive. Help the patient think positive thoughts. The mind and body fight back, too. And nutrition plays a significant part in recovery. The chemo fights the cancer. You need to fight the effects of chemotherapy."

"Your influence will help them afterwards, too. It will make their memories more precious."

"Memories? You mean he doesn't make it?"

"No, Christian, I'm sorry." He lowered his glance to the floor.

We stopped talking for the longest time.

So many cancer patients make it and live full lives. Some extend their time beyond all expectations. Yet some don't survive the ordeal. But new advances are being made every day. The earlier the detection, the better the odds.

Turning to me, Avery said, "I just need to point out two more people. The gentleman on the right just behind us. He heard you speak two years ago and decided that evening he, too, had to make a difference in the world. One year ago he started the on-line service over the Web that sends free positive messages twice weekly to anyone who wants them."

"I know his story," I said. "He e-mailed me recently to tell me that someone is copying the messages in the Netherlands and translating them to be sent out across Europe. He also mentioned one man who receives these same powerful words in Bosnia/Herzegovina and has started a Croatian version of that service."

"Finally you should recognize the gentlemen in the very last row. He has remained just out of sight during this trip."

"That's Bob. What's he doing here?" I asked.

"He's the one that paid the $10,000 to have you speak."

Bob and I met a few years ago and have basically been on the same mission. We have never been able to find the exact connection, but we believe there is something we are destined to do together. He is a very successful businessman with a deep commitment to people. He has spent a good portion of his personal fortune to help others.

"I have been truly blessed to have him as a friend, Avery."

"I know, Christian," he said.

"But why is he here? He's helped *me*. I have never been much of a help to him."

"You are so wrong, my friend. You provided the encouraging words he needed during the difficult times he's been through in this past year. His financial stability would never had been enough to get him through all of this. Money does not buy everything. But he is also here because he, too, is a Connector just like you. He often gets frustrated in his efforts to help people. When we land in Cleveland it will be his turn to discover people whom he has helped. You see, Christian, although you and Bob think you are working separately, you have been joined together by many of the same people. You have been both working together all along."

Avery then stood up, and looked at me and said, "I could fill a dozen planes with lives that have been touched by your actions. In fact, the average person influences more lives than one can measure. A dozen planes could easily be filled with people influenced by just one kindness. Multiply that by a lifetime and we've run out of planes. These are just a few of the people your life represents."

As he walked away an announcement came over the speaker that we were about to land in Cleveland. I gathered all of my belongings and, before I realized it, I was saying good-bye to my new friend.

"I can't tell you how much I appreciate this, Avery. I can see I do have a great deal more to accomplish. I will learn to trust more in God and less in the world. Success is the unseen miracles we all perform daily. I owe my life to you."

"No, Christian. Your son Kevin prayed for a miracle, and your son Kile is one. Go. You have a mission to fulfill."

I walked toward the terminal, up the long walkway. Just as I closed the door to the arrival gate I remembered I had left my notebook on the plane. The door was locked. I went to the desk and asked the attendant to open the door. I explained my predicament and showed her my boarding pass.

"Mr. Tyler, US Air flight #22 arrived several hours ago and has since continued its flight onto other destinations."

"No, I wasn't on US Air flight 22. It was Celestial Air. I just got off the plane a few minutes ago," I said

"Sir, I'm sorry. Your tickets and boarding pass indicate that you were definitely on US Air. May I suggest that you go to gate 33 and check in. Your connection for LaCrosse will be leaving in about 20 minutes."

I walked over to the window to get a closer look at the walkway leading to where I had just landed. There was nothing.

I quickly headed towards my next gate so I would not miss the final portion of my trip. Upon check-in the attendant told me that there was a message for me. The note simply said: "Have a safe trip. Your notebook will be on your seat. Avery"

Just as he had said, my notebook was there on aisle seat row 11. After take-off I reached for the notebook to finish the speech I was to give that evening. There on the tablet was my completed speech. Attached was a note that said "A little help from a friend."

That evening I spoke to *Families Can Survive*. I told them my personal story, from the day I lost my job to the gift of cancer. I concluded with the following written by a Scavenger friend of mine:

In This Day . . .

I choose living not just for the sake of passing time.

I choose to take advantage of the milli-seconds between my breath and my sigh.

In this day I will grasp hold of the moments I lost so many times before as harsh words rolled off my tongue penetrating the ears and hearts of those whom I wanted to hurt and did.

In this day I will make up for time lost by living between my thoughts and my actions. I will live up to my potential which, through God's Grace is unlimited.

In this day I will help someone else find the greatest gift of all-himself. While we spend our lives in pursuit of success and happiness, we have within ourselves all that we will ever need from the moment of conception until our last breath.

In this day I will acknowledge that I am a magnificent creation capable of the greatest accomplishments. I am one of a kind. Never before in the history of human existence and never again will there be another me. I have a purpose, a mission, and with that a responsibility to fulfill my goals. The key to success is in "knowing" and "believing" that I can, then purposefully taking action. The "knowing" is the small voice you hear deep within that gives direction. It sparks the dreams and softens the indignant blows that life throws at us. It is the spirit of our being connected to the Great Power. It never goes away, although many spend a lifetime trying to block it out. "Believing" comes once we have accepted that self esteem is not an ego trip but a verification that you are a living miracle created by God. Although we are all capable of grand accomplishments that can change the world, we can all succeed at various levels none less important than the next. Some listen more intently to the inner voice and act upon their beliefs.

Others cautiously follow, taking life step by step. Even those who do not heed the call serve a purpose. They often serve as the best friend, the parent, the neighbor, who ignites the spark in others bound for greater goals.

In this day I will celebrate as if it was my birthday and 24 hours was my gift. I will treasure the sunrise, and save the light in my hand for darkened days. I will fill my lungs to capacity with the sweet smell of life and consume the colors that surround me like a meal fit for a king. I will taste the reds and yellows of the flowers, and bathe in the blues and greens of the sky and grass. At the end of the day, in the darkest hours, my soul will light the way to rest in the satisfaction of knowing I did not waste a morsel.

Then on my last day on this earth I will leave filled with joy to a better place, knowing that I have served my purpose and completed my mission. I will leave behind my energy that will disperse into every rock, tree and molecule. I will become a part of the color, the light, the breath of life for others to consume. I will not wither to the ground as a failure, and serve as a pathway. I will rise with the sun to bring joy forever to those who will dream after me.

I am important. I am successful. I am God's creation!
I am Alive!

The roar of the crowd was overwhelming. I had never before had a response like that. I was on fire with hope, and filled with passion to return home to those I loved and to begin again. When I got to my room at the hotel the message light was blinking on my phone. I called the operator and she said a man had stopped by. There was a message from him at the front desk. Also Michele had called and wanted me to call home immediately.

I called Michele before going to the front desk.

"Is there anything wrong?" I asked anxiously.

"Wrong? The only thing that's wrong is you need a secretary," she said.

"A secretary for what?" I asked.

"There must be five agents who have called since you left. Some have several dates they want confirmed, and others need more video tapes from you. Come home now!" she said, laughing.

I couldn't believe it. This all had to be a dream. My life. My life was back on track. I couldn't wait to get home. I couldn't wait to hold Michele again, and see my two sons.

I ran down to the front desk and retrieved the message. It was a small envelope addressed to me from A. More.

This wasn't a dream . He did exist. I had his note in my hand. I opened it, and in large print was:

***"I believe in YOU!'* Ever more!"**

Afterword

Where you are right now in life is your choice.

Let your dreams take flight!
Join me on a journey of change . . .
Celestial Air Flight #22 is now boarding!

I do hope that you have enjoyed the book. Most of what you have read actually happened. Perhaps you have experienced similar events and you have decisions to make right now. Sometimes in life the right choices are clear. Many times we muddy our vision with negative thoughts or permit "ego" to rule over what's "right." Ultimately your life is your choice.

If you are not at all happy with where you are, then somewhere along the way you made a poor decision or you have given up control of your life to others. Are you a failure? No! Let me remind you once again that failure is an event not a person.

Creating your "Life Map"

The flight we are about to make together will take you on a voyage similar to Christian Tyler's. But before we go you'll need to prepare a flight plan. So please get a pencil and a sheet of paper.

Don't say it. Don't tell yourself "I don't have time

right now. I'll do this later." I promise you will never get to it. So do it now. It will only take a few minutes.

In order to understand where you want to go (the goal setting principles we discussed in the book) you first need to understand where you are. Our journey to the land of "Change" will require the creation of your "Life Map." Don't worry, you do not need to be an artist. You see, this map is filled with circles all connected to you in the center. Easy enough?

First place the paper horizontally in front of you. Draw a small circle in the middle and write your name in it. (See figure 1)

Next, draw a circle to the right and write "Family" in it. Surround the "Family" circle with smaller ones that represent each immediate member. Draw a straight line from your name over to the "Family" circle. Draw another circle to the left of your name and write "Friends" in it and surround it with small circles and names. Draw a straight line from your name to the "Friends" circle.

We are beginning to form a pattern. There you are, in the center with family to the right and friends to the left. These are just a few of the people who depend on you. These are the lives that you know you influence everyday.

Finally, draw another circle and label it "Work" and surround it with co-workers and their names. Continue this process by adding circles labeled "Beliefs," "Hobbies," "Goals," etc.

Draw straight lines from your name to each major circle. Add sheets of paper in any direction so that you get a complete overview of your life. Have fun and be creative.

When you are finished, lay the "Life Map" out on a large table or on the floor. Looking down on this map is like looking out of the window in an airplane. Below we see highways connecting homes and businesses, in communities connected by governments, in states connected by highways, in countries connected by boats and trains and planes. All of it connected by our Creator.

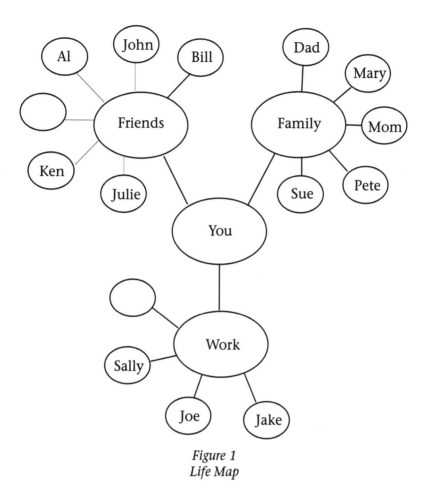

Figure 1
Life Map

Every one of the people listed on your "Life Map" are the center in *their* world. Your influence on them is multiplied outward to the people they touch. In turn, they are each the center of a world far beyond your reach but directly influenced by your life. Picture a field with thousands of "Life Maps" intertwined. Then picture more fields touching that one.

Your one act of kindness sends a ripple into lives you

will never see. Your caring words to a neighbor brightens his day so that his spirit is lifted and in feeling so, treats his daughter to kind words or acts. She then, enlightened by the experience, takes it home to a friend, who at just the right moment, feels good enough about herself to decide to take that college course she dreamed of, so that she can get a better job. This goes on to infinity.

How do you feel about what you see? Have you discovered *your circle of influence?* Are there areas that need more circles?

You have the ability to change your map and add to or take away from areas that concern you. Don't wait for people to come into your life. Go out in search for those people you would like to call friends or associates. Your map will need constant updating.

Let's move on to the next step. My ultimate challenge to you.

Create your "Passenger List"

The flight that is now boarding will be filled with people you have influenced in your life. Make up a passenger list of names and stories. Write down as many people as you can think of using the "Life Map" you created earlier.

Stop it! I can hear that doubt rumbling through your negative mind. You, my friend, can fill this plane and many more. I guarantee it.

Start with your friends, neighbors, family, and all of the obvious choices. Then expand your list to the mailman, the waitress at your favorite diner, the grocery clerk, and the unknown recipient of the note of thanks you sent when paying the department store bill by mail. Stretch your memory back to earlier days and don't be shy.

If you must, set the passenger list aside for now. We're in no hurry to leave. Come back to it an hour from now or tomorrow and take notes all day as you begin to remember all the ways you have touched the lives of those around you.

Now look at your map. Look at your passenger list. *You are important!* Take charge of your life, now. Develop your goals and take action. Use the list of people and the "Life Map" as contacts to help you accomplish your dreams.

There are things that you can do everyday to keep your spirits high and your goals on track. Just like an airplane you need to create a plan, a check list everyday before you head out into the world.

Along the way you'll need to make adjustments. When a plane leaves New York headed to California, it doesn't take a direct flight to get there. Depending on air traffic and weather conditions the pilot will be off course more times than on. Many of the changes occur during the flight and are not pre-planned. The same concept is needed in life.

Don't complicate your plans with too many details. This simple formula, "Your Ten Step Daily Flight Plan," is a great way to get yourself started. Personalize it with ideas and activities that will make it enjoyable for you. It takes work to make life fun.

Your Ten Step Daily Flight Plan

1. Start first with a word of thanks to your Creator.
2. Read the speech *"In This Day"* when you awaken each morning.
3. Review your daily goals written the evening before.

4. Plan to make a difference in someone's life today with a simple act of kindness.
5. Do everything bigger and brighter than expected. Go the extra mile.
6. Take care of your body. Eat healthy to provide the fuel your body needs. Drink eight glasses of water and add a half teaspoon of salt to your food. Avoid all caffeine because it is a diuretic. Your body is mostly water. Dehydration is the cause of many major diseases.
7. In the evening feed your mind. Read another chapter from a book designed to help you grow. Support your local library and discover the classic self help books from long ago.
8. Make time for your family. They are an important part of who you are.
9. Review your goals from today and set new ones for tomorrow.
10. Before going to sleep, say thanks to your Creator.

Remember "I Believe in YOU!"
God Bless!

"The Flight of a Lifetime!" Seminar . . .

The same life changing principles that have been presented in this book are available in an exciting three hour seminar.

This interactive, entertaining program will help attendees:

*Develop goals and set priorities (**Flight Plan**)
*Take inventory of their strengths and talents (**Preflight Checklist**)
*Create a network of support at work and home (**Ground Crew**)
*Review their "Circle of Influence" (**Passenger List**)
And more exciting life changing activities.

Experience this program from take off to landing

Take your employees, club or organization to new heights. Help them to discover the significant roles they play in work and in their personal life.

Robert C. Perks is an author, professional speaker, trainer, and a member of the *National Speakers Association*. Bob has addressed meetings and conferences across the U.S. He is host of a weekly radio show "Success Line" and former television host on PBS.

Contact Creative Motivation at
717-696-2581 Phone
717-696-1310 Fax

"I Believe in YOU!" Newsletter

Making important life changes requires planning, goal setting, and daily positive affirmation of our self worth.

Now you can receive a bi-monthly newsletter filled with positive stories and ideas. Each issue will include:

"Standing on the shoulders of giants"—inspirational quotes

Guest feature articles—life stories, health issues for women and men

"Taking action"—lessons in goal setting, stress management, time management and more.

"Ever more"—poems and stories from our readers

"**A view from the road**"—stories of hope and messages of love from people I meet while doing seminars and speaking engagements.

Send $15.00 check or money order, payable to ***Sparrow Publishing*** for a full year subscription (6 issues) to:

Sparrow Publishing
88 North Pioneer Ave.
Shavertown, Pa. 18708

Available from Sparrow Publishing . . .

"The Flight of a Lifetime" by Robert C. Perks, paperback
_____ copies at $9.95 each   Total $ _____

The *"I Believe in You!"* bracelet
As featured in the book, this leather bracelet, with colorful plastic beads comes with the beautiful sentiment describing each bead and makes an excellent gift for a friend or a reminder for you of how very important you are in life.
_____ bracelets at $5.00 each   Total $ _____

Audio tape: *"I believe in you!/ On the shoulders of giants"*
A powerful inspirational message from Robert C. Perks, author and motivational speaker. Side two includes stories and quotes from some of the greatest minds in history.
_____ tapes at $8.00 each   Total $ _____
Subtotal $ _____
Pa. residents add 6% sales tax $ _____
Shipping add $2.00 for each item ordered $ _____
Total $ _____

Please ship to:

Name_____

Phone _____

Address _____

City _____State _____Zip_____

Make checks or money order payable to:

Sparrow Publishing.
88 North Pioneer Ave.
Shavertown, Pa. 18708

Please allow two weeks for delivery.

**Call 717-696-2581 for a list of other books
and tapes available.**